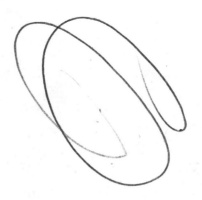

ORCHESTRAL CONDUCTING

A TEXTBOOK
FOR STUDENTS AND AMATEURS

BY

ADAM CARSE
FELLOW OF THE ROYAL ACADEMY OF MUSIC

GREENWOOD PRESS, PUBLISHERS
WESTPORT, CONNECTICUT

Originally published in 1929
by Augener Ltd., London

First Greenwood Reprinting 1971

Library of Congress Catalogue Card Number 78-109716

SBN 8371-4206-7

Printed in the United States of America

CONTENTS

PART I

THE TECHNIQUE OF CONDUCTING

PART II

THE INSTRUMENTS OF THE ORCHESTRA

iii

CONTENTS

PART III

ORCHESTRAL CONDUCTING

PART I
THE TECHNIQUE OF CONDUCTING

INTRODUCTION

THE purpose of what follows is to deal with the technique of orchestral conducting, and with the instruments of the orchestra in so far as a conductor should understand them ; no attempt is made to consider the art from the interpretive point of view, nor does choral conducting come within the scope of these pages.

The advice given is offered to the growing number of students who undergo a course of training as conductors at the larger schools of music ; to the many amateurs who conduct orchestras, yet have had little or no opportunity of studying the technical side of the art—in other words, to those who conduct by the light of nature ; and to a large class who, although they are professional musicians, are, at the same time, only amateur conductors.

In Part I. the handling of the baton and the physical movements of the conductor are considered, always, be it understood, as a means of controlling or influencing in some way or other the playing of the orchestra ; for, as conductors may easily forget, no sort of physical movement is justified unless it conveys something to the players under their control, and then only when the players respond to that movement. A conductor will be judged by the playing of his orchestra , not by the amount of physical energy he displays ; not through the *eyes* but through the *ears* of his audience. When a conductor finishes a piece with a crumpled collar, wildly disarranged hair, and showing every sign of complete physical exhaustion, these *may* all be thoroughly justified if the orchestra has played the piece well ; if not, the energy expended has been ineffectual, and therefore misdirected. The applause that follows the performance of a piece may be given because the conductor has caused his orchestra to play well, but not because he has reduced his body and mind to a state of limp exhaustion. Conducting *is* playing on an orchestra as on an instrument ;

playing is the physical exertion without which music cannot be made to sound, and sound is something which is *heard*; conducting, therefore, should be aimed at the aural, and not at the visual sense.

Following an exposition on the physical side of his functions, an attempt is made to aid the student in acquiring a part of the conductor's equipment which may be epigrammatically described as being almost of more importance than the conducting itself; that is, the rehearsing or preparing of an orchestra for a performance. That aspect of the subject must necessarily include much that is not concerned with, nor expressed by, mere physical movement. To make the most of the time available for rehearsal is to contribute at least as much towards the excellence of the playing as anything that can be done during the actual performance. The conductor who can rehearse well is the one who can *hear* well, and who hearing, knows what to do. Modern methods of piano teaching lay great stress on the importance of *listening*; this is equally important to the conductor who is rehearsing, for till he has *heard* he cannot *act* effectually.

The parallel between a player playing on an instrument and a conductor *playing* on an orchestra serves very well up to a point; it breaks down when it is followed up so far as the point where the connection between the player and the instrument steps in. The player acts directly on his instrument; the conductor acts on his orchestra only through the intermediacy of a *number of players* who are playing on a *variety of instruments*. The knowledge of what these players can do with their instruments is of as much importance to a conductor as the knowledge to an individual player of what he can do on his particular instrument. The conductor has to direct the player how to play, and the more he knows about the player's instrument the more effectually will he be able to direct the playing on it. Part II., therefore, is devoted to the instruments of the orchestra, to the principles by which they produce their sounds, to the mechanical means by which these sounds are controlled, and to the limitations and individualities of the several types which go to make up the large composite but human instrument which we call an orchestra.

The principles governing string technique are sufficiently well understood by many embryo conductors who have some practical experience of string playing. Wind-instrument technique is a closed book to a very large proportion of those who cheerfully assume the responsibility of telling wind players how to play, or to some who are so conscious of the handicap of their ignorance that they therefore refrain from giving directions to the players on those instruments. Many are content to regard wind instruments as strange contrivances which, by some mysterious means, can produce quite a large number of sounds by the operation of a surprisingly small number of mechanical keys. The Sections III., IV., and V. of Part II. are designed with the intention, or the hope, of enlightening the minds of such as ask wonderingly of a trumpet player, "However can you play so many different notes when you have got only three keys on your instrument?"

Section VII. just touches in the most essential particulars on the ground which in most textbooks on orchestration is more amply covered ; at least one comprehensive treatise on the subject should be in the possession of every aspiring conductor.

In Part III. a short history of the growth of conducting as a specialized branch of musical activity is appended, which, with a Bibliography, the author ventures to hope, will stimulate interest in a field which is by no means too well provided with literature.

SECTION I

THE BEAT

THE direction in which the baton moves is the means by which a player in an orchestra knows which beat of the bar is approaching ; time-beating, therefore, is based on direction, and four directions are possible—viz., downwards, upwards, to the left, and to the right. The down-beat has always been associated with the first beat, or strongest accent, in the bar, and the up-beat with the last.

Music normally requires either two, three, or four beats in a bar, and these are shown by motions of the conductor's baton in the following directions :

Duple Time (Two Beats).

1.	2.
Down	Up.

Triple Time (Three Beats).

1.	2.	3.
Down	Right	Up.

Quadruple Time (Four Beats).

1.	2.	3.	4.
Down	Left	Right	Up.

The above are the three fundamental methods of time-beating, of which all others are modifications to suit a quick or a slow pace (*tempo*), and which may involve taking two or three beats as one in the case of quick *tempi*, or the subdividing of each beat into halves or thirds in the case of slow *tempi*—the halves for simple time, and the thirds for compound time. Thus, if the bars in duple or in triple time are so short in duration that it is impracticable to give each beat separately, each bar will be given only one beat, and that a down-beat; on the same principle, in a quadruple bar which is too quick for four beats, only the first and third beats are given, and these will be down- and up-beats, just as in duple time; in fact, a quick quadruple time becomes in practice a duple time: $\frac{4}{4}$ becomes $\frac{2}{2}$, $\frac{4}{8}$ becomes $\frac{2}{4}$, and so on.

When the *tempo* is slow it may be necessary to subdivide the beat; in the case of a slow duple-simple time—that is, when four beats are necessary—the ordinary way of beating four in a bar can be adopted; thus, a slow $\frac{2}{4}$ time becomes in practice a $\frac{4}{8}$ time. But in the case of slow triple or quadruple times, when six or eight beats respectively are required, the subdivision is carried out as follows:

Slow Triple-Simple Time.

1. $\begin{cases}(a) \text{ Down} \\ (b) \text{ Down}\end{cases}$ 2. $\begin{cases}(a) \text{ Right} \\ (b) \text{ Right}\end{cases}$ 3. $\begin{cases}(a) \text{ Up.} \\ (b) \text{ Up.}\end{cases}$

Slow Quadruple-Simple Time.

1. $\begin{cases}(a) \text{ Down} \\ (b) \text{ Down}\end{cases}$ 2. $\begin{cases}(a) \text{ Left} \\ (b) \text{ Left}\end{cases}$ 3. $\begin{cases}(a) \text{ Right} \\ (b) \text{ Right}\end{cases}$ 4. $\begin{cases}(a) \text{ Up.} \\ (b) \text{ Up.}\end{cases}$

Slow Triple-Compound Time.

1. $\begin{cases}(a) \text{ Down} \\ (b) \text{ Down} \\ (c) \text{ Down}\end{cases}$ 2. $\begin{cases}(a) \text{ Right} \\ (b) \text{ Right} \\ (c) \text{ Right}\end{cases}$ 3. $\begin{cases}(a) \text{ Up.} \\ (b) \text{ Up.} \\ (c) \text{ Up.}\end{cases}$

Slow Quadruple-Compound Time.

1. $\begin{cases}(a) \text{ Down} \\ (b) \text{ Down} \\ (c) \text{ Down}\end{cases}$ 2. $\begin{cases}(a) \text{ Left} \\ (b) \text{ Left} \\ (c) \text{ Left}\end{cases}$ 3. $\begin{cases}(a) \text{ Right} \\ (b) \text{ Right} \\ (c) \text{ Right}\end{cases}$ 4. $\begin{cases}(a) \text{ Up.} \\ (b) \text{ Up.} \\ (c) \text{ Up.}\end{cases}$

In making the subdivided beats in slow *tempi*, the second (or in compound times the second and third) motion in each beat should be distinctly "smaller"; that is to say, in approaching them the baton does not move so far, nor so quickly, as it does when making the main or real beat, but the duration must, of course, be the same in all cases. The "smaller" beats are really repetitions of the main beats on a smaller scale, so that the general principle of "direction" is still preserved.

Quick, or moderately quick, compound-duple times $(\frac{6}{4}, \frac{6}{8}, \frac{6}{16})$ will, of course, be done exactly as in the case of their corresponding simple-duple times; but when the *tempo* is slow enough to require a subdivided beat, the following is a usual method:

Slow Duple-Compound Time.

1. $\begin{cases}(a) \text{ Down} \\ (b) \text{ Left} \\ (c) \text{ Left}\end{cases}$ 2. $\begin{cases}(a) \text{ Right.} \\ (b) \text{ Right.} \\ (c) \text{ Up.}\end{cases}$

Music of five beats in a bar is usually grouped as either $2+3$ or $3+2$, and, although there are several ways of beating five, the following may be taken as samples which carry out the general principles of time-beating:

Five Beats $(2+3)$.

1. Down	2. Left	3. Right	4. Right	5. Up.

Five Beats $(3+2)$.

1. Down	2. Left	3. Left	4. Right	5. Up.

Seven beats in a bar admits of still more variety of treatment, yet will always be clearer if the principle of the subdivided beat be adopted; the two main differences will be when the beats are grouped as either $3+4$ or as $4+3$:

Seven Beats $(3+4)$.

1. Down	2. Left 3. Left	4. Right 5. Right	6. Up. 7. Up.

Or

1. Down 2. Down	3. Left	4. Right 5. Right	6. Up. 7. Up.

Seven Beats (4 + 3).

1. Down	3. Left	5. Right	
2. Down	4. Left	6. Right	7. Up.

Or

1. Down	3. Left		6. Up.
2. Down	4. Left	5. Right	7. Up.

The questions whether a beat should be subdivided, or whether two or three beats should be reduced to one, depends on the speed at which the music is played, and it rests with the conductor to decide which is the most suitable, and to make his decision known to the orchestra. A lot of short, quick motions of the baton are difficult to follow and are apt to confuse; on the other hand, fewer very long motions are difficult to keep steady. For *tempi* which are just on the border-line between quick-short and slow-long beats, it will generally be advisable to decide on the slow-long beat.

Conductors will occasionally subdivide some particular beat of a bar while leaving the others undivided; this will generally occur in moderately slow *tempi* in order to either broaden or emphasize a note of shorter value than the beat itself. A compromise between a subdivided and an undivided beat is often useful in quick triple times (such as waltz times, for example) when the *tempo* is too quick for three separate beats. The device is to give only one down-beat for the first two-thirds of the bar, and then a distinct up-beat for the last. A tendency to hurry or "run away," on the part of either conductor or orchestra, or both, may be checked by this means.

It should be understood that the above directions are all taken from the conductor's standpoint, and that to a player facing him they will, of course, be reversed as far as the player's right or left side are concerned; this, however, offers no difficulty to the player, who is accustomed to seeing them thus reversed, and associates the sideways beats with their directions as seen from his own point of view.

The practice of saying or of shouting out the number of the beats in a bar is one which may be difficult to resist when handling sluggish players during rehearsal, but is best avoided altogether, as it only too easily becomes a habit and leads players to rely on *hearing* the beat instead of on *seeing* it. Hammering on the desk or music with the baton, also the still worse habit of stamping out the time with the foot, are similar appeals to the ear instead of to the eye, and, for the reason just given, should not be allowed to become part of a conductor's means of controlling or of stimulating his players.

Time-beating can be practised alone, or to music played on a piano or on a gramophone, till the student makes the movements automatically, that is, without having to *think* of the directions in which the baton moves.

Some conductors, if closely watched, will sometimes be found to be making more than one down-beat in a bar; it may even be said without exaggeration that there are occasions when conductors who are obviously fully competent appear to use no other than a down-beat, and with apparently quite satisfactory results. This method of beating may serve well enough when an experienced conductor is handling an orchestra the members of which are accustomed to play under his direction and know his ways well, or when the music which is being played is familiar to all concerned. Under these circumstances it may not be necessary for a conductor to distinguish between the first and the other beats of the bar; as long as some sort of a beat is distinctly given, the *tempo* and *ensemble* may be successfully preserved, and by their own metrical feeling the players may keep well together, while the conductor "plays on the orchestra" in a sense which has nothing to do with the preservation of mere metrical precision.

That this "down-beat conducting" is sometimes successfully carried out should not be interpreted by the student as a recommendation to beat anyhow and anywhere; in music which is metrically very straightforward and runs on its course without interruption, it is not absolutely essential that a conductor's time-beat should distinguish between the various beats of the bar, because the players can quite well feel the regular recurrence of the strong accent, and are not likely to lose sight of it; but when the metre is not very clearly and regularly marked, when any sort of liberty is to be taken with the time, when it is liable to interruption, and when the rhythm is at all irregular, the use of more than one down-beat in a bar is dangerous, and may easily produce an untidy *ensemble* or lead to the hesitation or confusion which is almost bound to arise when players feel uncertain as to the recurrence of the first beat of the bar.

SECTION II

STARTING POSITION

JUST before beginning to beat time it is necessary to prepare the orchestra for the start by assuming an attitude, and by holding the baton steady for a few moments, in a position which commands attention. This attitude should be one which suggests authority without being unnecessarily assertive or threatening in manner; the idea should be rather more that of an invitation to which a ready response is confidently expected. The baton is held with the point slanting upwards and the right hand about level with, but to the right of, the conductor's chest. As the baton will always have to rise still higher before making the first beat, it is unadvisable to hold it too high up before leaving the starting position; on the other hand, if held too low down, the motion of the baton may not be clearly seen, or the general attitude may fail to secure the proper attention of the players. Whichever beat of the bar is to be given first, the baton should be made to move away from the starting position with a slowish curved motion, almost as if revolving round the starting-point, and to rise upwards with accumulating speed. This is all preliminary to the actual first beat, and it is important that this motion should be ample in scope and deliberate in action, so that when the first beat is made the players are not taken by surprise. A quick angular action is sure to fail in securing a unanimous start owing to the players being unable to judge correctly the moment when the first beat is due. In the Figures 1, 2, and 3, the stationary starting position is marked A, from whence the curved path of the hand and baton can easily be followed.

When about to begin, a conductor should look comprehensively over the whole orchestra, or, if only some of the players are concerned with the start, towards that particular group; his attention should be directed *to the orchestra*, and *not to the full score* in front of him.

Before beginning, a conductor will generally have to concentrate his mind for a few moments on the coming *tempo* (speed). When faced with the responsibility of setting it, the inexperienced conductor will probably realize how much more difficult it is to actually decide on than to criticize a *tempo*. A broad view of the whole movement rather than only the very beginning, and perhaps a bar or two mentally counted, will help towards a decision which, however, may be subject to slight readjustment during the course of the first few bars.

On the whole, it will be found more difficult to reduce the speed of a quick movement which has been started a little too fast than to increase the speed when the start has been a little on the slow side.

SECTION III

ACTION

THE actual handling of the baton in beating time should aim at making quite clear to the players which beat of the bar is coming next, and, what is even more important, *when it is coming*.

Every action of the conductor is in curves, and all angles made in the air are spherical angles. The beginning of each beat should have a distinctly marked and rather sharp movement of the baton, one which indicates the exact moment when the motion of the baton from the previous beat culminates in the arrival of the new beat. This movement, in which a flexible wrist must take part, is of a rather elastic nature, and may look as if the point of the baton had met with some springy resistance which had sent it off in the direction of the next beat. It is brought about by increasing the speed at which the baton moves through the air just before the incidence of the new beat. In slow *legato* playing, the nature of that culminating movement will usually become rather less jerky, and takes on more of a gentle or rounded character, as if the obstruction met with were of a very spongy nature, but must, nevertheless, be sufficiently marked to show quite clearly the moment when the new beat occurs. The actual physical movement made at the moment of the beat varies more or less with different conductors and with the varying nature of the music being played, but all follow the general *directions* indicated in Section I. A beat may be approached from a higher or a lower level, the baton may make a sharp spherical angle in the air or may be the lowest point of a curve, yet will be clearly either up, down, to the left or to the right of the conductor.

In between the beats the baton should be *always in motion*, slowly or quickly according to the amount of time occupied between the beats ; it should never be allowed to come to a complete standstill, except, of course, when there is some actual interruption in the progress of the music, such as occurs, for example, at a pause. The beginner's usual mistake is to move the baton as if trying to hit a series of imaginary objects in the air, and as if endeavouring to get from one object to another by the shortest route possible, and then to remain at each spot for some time before moving off to hit at the next object. These imaginary objects in the air *must not be taken by surprise*, because, if they are, the players in the orchestra will also be taken by surprise. Sudden darts on the part of the baton from one stationary position to another cannot be mentally anticipated by the players; they will be the cause of a bad *ensemble* which takes the form of playing just *after* the beat. The idea should be, not to make the players *follow* the conductor's beat—just as a poor accompanist trails after a soloist—but to make them play *with* the conductor.

The motion from beat to beat should be gradual but cumulative in speed, so that the player can judge exactly when the baton is due to arrive at the beginning of the next beat. To achieve this, all the joints concerned—namely, the knuckles, wrist, elbow, and shoulder—must be in a free and flexible condition, so that no movement is angular or sudden, and no position fixed or rigid. All the curved movements of the baton from beat to beat have a general tendency to rise in between the beats, to fall towards the actual moment of the beat, and then to rise again, while still maintaining their general movements in the four cardinal directions—up, down, left or right.

The actual size of the curves largely depends on the duration of time between the beats, and on whether one is trying to get much or little tone from the orchestra. Slow *tempi* will tend to amplify the extent of the curves, while quick *tempi* necessarily restrict their scope. Loud, rich tone requires a large, broad action, and little tone a smaller one.

The Figures 1, 2, and 3, will give some idea of the curved actions of a conductor's hand when in motion. They are actual photographic records of the progress of a hand through the air, and, although not to be taken as the precise movements made by every conductor, will show sufficiently clearly how free from anything approaching angularity is the path traced by a conductor's hand and baton. In each case a start was made from the stationary position marked A; the beats occur approximately at the points indicated by the numerals, and the whole is broken off at the point where the hand reaches its greatest height previous to falling towards the next down-beat.

The smaller movements of the baton are made with the wrist, or even with the fingers, then, as the radius extends, the elbow and shoulder joints are brought into action.

Another matter which will govern the extent of a conductor's actions is the size of the orchestra, and, arising out of that, the distance between the players and the conductor. It is true that experienced conductors, when handling professional orchestras, can to some extent dispense with formal time-beating altogether and devote their actions to aiding the interpretation of the music. Anything but a first-class orchestra

FIG. 1.   FIG. 2.

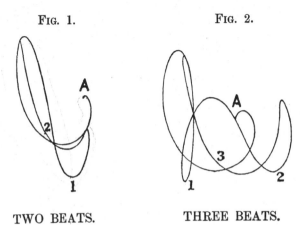

TWO BEATS.   THREE BEATS.

FIG. 3.

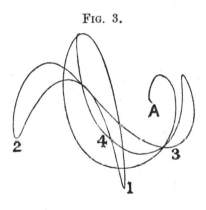

FOUR BEATS.

under experienced control, however, requires a clear and constant time-beat, and conductors of such, more especially when they have not much experience to build on, are recommended to cultivate at first a straightforward beat of moderate dimensions, free from unnecessary elaboration, ambiguity, or exaggeration. Their forces are not usually very large, and no great amount of tone can be extracted from small orchestras ; the beat which is required to control a choir and orchestra in the Albert Hall is not necessary in a school hall or cinema theatre where the platform or space available for an orchestra is small and the players are few in number. It is unnecessarily fatiguing, and looks rather ridiculous if the movements of the conductor of a Handel Festival are reproduced in a village hall.

The area in which the baton moves about is that which lies roughly in front of and to the right side of the conductor's chest and face. Observation will prove that it is impossible to lay down a definite line below or above which the right hand should not travel, for in practice it will be found that it may descend to as low as the waist or as high as above the head, yet a circle with a diameter of about two and a half feet will cover all the normal movements of a conductor's right hand. If a beat is consistently made too low down, say, on a level with the waist, it will not be seen by all the players, and if made too high up, will not be seen with any comfort by players seated near to the conductor, and, incidentally, will prove very exhausting to the latter. The conductor's music-desk should not be so high as to invade the space where the baton moves. A high desk will cause a conductor either to beat too much on his right side, where the movements cannot be easily seen by players on his left, or to beat so high up as to be uncomfortable and tiring to the arm.

Comparatively little movement of the body is necessary when conducting. There should be no sort of stiffness which will interfere with free action of the arms, and the body must be free to turn to the right or the left. An ordinary, natural and upright posture is the normal attitude, with an inclination to bend forward when required, such as, for example, in order to soften the tone or to pick out some particular part of the orchestra for special attention. Otherwise, the body will turn easily to right or left when the attention of a particular player or group of players is required. The feet need not remain absolutely fixed and stationary during the performance of an entire piece, but restless movements of the feet, or anything approaching "walking about," is better avoided as a habit, if only for the reason that if one walks away from the central position one has to spend so much time in walking back again, and attention may be lost during the return journey. Rising on the toes and bending at the knees are also unnecessary movements which are better checked before they become habits.

The grasp of the baton will naturally vary according to whether the beat is given firmly and with emphasis, or quietly and unobtrusively ; on the whole, it is held rather loosely, as if hinged, between the thumb and index finger, and should not be "clutched" or appear to be held as if one intended to hit some invisible foe as hard as possible. It is a matter for each individual to settle for himself which particular pattern of baton is used. Some attention should be paid to the balance, but otherwise individual taste and comfort in handling it will decide whether the baton should be provided with a bulb, a cork handle, or nothing at all at the end which is held in the hand. At the present time a very light and thin baton is almost universally used.

SECTION IV

Gesture

The action of the conductor's arm and baton should, of course, not aim at being merely a sort of human metronome, the object of which is concerned only with metrical precision. The character of the beat, the conductor's attitude and facial expression, and his left hand and arm, these are all used to convey to the players the various shades of loud and soft, the rise and fall of tone or *tempo*, the style and feeling—in short, all that goes to make up the rendering of a piece of music. The left hand is an especially useful help in indicating the manner of performance apart from the mere speed. Too much use of the left hand, however, cancels its own value, because the players soon become accustomed to seeing it always on the move, and, taking that as the normal procedure, are apt to become unresponsive to its signs and directions. The left hand that is always in action, particularly when it only repro-duces the movements of the right hand in reversed directions, might as well not be used at all. *Nothing is gained by beating time in duplicate;* indeed, much is lost, because the conductor whose left hand also beats time is depriving himself of his most valuable means of indicating expression, light and shade, and many other features which the right hand cannot show. The left hand should rather be kept in reserve for particular situa-tions when they do arise : to give special emphasis, to do what the time-beating hand is unable to do, to draw attention, and generally to aid in the interpretation of the music ; it will be useless for any of these purposes if the left hand is kept constantly on the move.

What has been said of the over-use of the left hand applies very generally to all conductor's gestures. The conductor who is continually gesticulating is wasting his reserves ; the players will be sure to ignore some of his too many signs, and the result will be that the audience *see* a fussy conductor, but *hear* only a colourless performance. Further, when gestures follow one another in close succession, they are liable to be too sudden, and therefore too late for any response from the players. After all, music is not perpetually changing its expression and manner ; not every bar is charged with special effects, nor every beat with some telling point. The feeling may remain level for some time; no alteration in the manner of performance may be required for longer or shorter periods, and the conductor, once the right spirit has been established, need not fear that the performance is going to suffer, or that his ability as a conductor will be questioned because he does not keep on displaying a constantly varied selection of physical movements. *A conductor should be always mentally on the alert, but should not appear to be in a state of perpetual agitation.*

Certain gestures are the common property of all conductors, while others are the habits or even the mannerisms of individuals. The raising of the left hand with the palm downwards is generally used to subdue the amount of tone ; this gesture may be directed so as to cover the whole orchestra or only to particular players for the purpose of adjusting the balance of tone. The hand rising with the palm turned inwards or upwards will tend to increase the tone, while such as a clenched fist will indicate special force or vigour ; even the fingers of the left hand may be brought into use to give more delicate signs of a manner of performance than can be given by the hand which holds the baton.

Students and others in the embryonic stage are very apt to model their actions and gestures on those of prominent conductors. No better advice can be given to such than to recommend them to carefully differentiate between technique and mannerism, to study the technique of good conductors, but not to ape their mannerisms.

SECTION V

" GETTING HOLD OF THE ORCHESTRA "

Change of Speed.   Change of Time.

AN orchestra must always be aware that something is expected of it before the actual moment when that something is to occur ; thus, the progress of the baton *towards* a beat should prepare the players and enable them to feel when the beat is coming. *The same idea should underlie any other action of a conductor;* in fact, it may be taken as an all-round axiom that an orchestra cannot respond to any sudden movement of the conductor at the very moment when response is required; unless their attention is engaged beforehand, unless they are led to expect something, their response will fail, or it may come too late, or it may come piecemeal, with bad *ensemble* as the result. It is true, one sometimes sees conductors making sudden physical movements and an orchestra *apparently* responding to them with effect; but in·such cases it may be taken as quite certain that the effect would have been forthcoming *without* the physical movement.

There are several situations which commonly occur in orchestral playing when it is important that the players should have ample warning that their special attention is expected, and it is the duty of the conductor to give that warning in good time by means of a particular alertness in his attitude, by a look of expectancy, by a sort of "tightening of the reins" which will give him a firmer hold on the players' attention. These situations occur particularly : (*a*) when the speed is to be increased or decreased, or when any sort of liberty is to be taken with the usual regularity of the beat ; (*b*) when either the *tempo* or the time is to be changed ; (*c*) when special emphasis is required ; (*d*) when the *tempo* is to be established at the beginning of a piece or movement ; (*e*) when the regular recurrence of the beat is to be held up by a pause ; (*f*) when any particular player or group of players are to make an important entry or "lead."

The first (*a*), indicated by such terms as *rallentando* or *accelerando*, meaning respectively a *gradual* lengthening or shortening of the duration of the beat, require that the conductor should first get hold of the attention of the orchestra, and, with his eyes on the players and *not* on the score, should gradually *bend* the speed in the required direction. If this is done without any sort of warning, the response may be late or the *ensemble* may suffer. The conductor should note whether these changes of speed are to be made at a quick or at a slow rate, so that they will last out the period they are intended to cover, and not exhaust their effect at too early a stage.

When a quickening of speed continues to such an extent that it becomes necessary to reduce the number of beats in a bar—say, from six quaver-beats to two dotted crotchet-beats ($\frac{6}{8}$ *Adagio* to $\frac{6}{8}$ *Allegro*)—the moment at which the change of beat-value is to be made requires careful selection and a baton movement which cannot be misunderstood. At that moment it is particularly necessary that the conductor should have a firm "hold of the orchestra," so that the sudden change from a rapid to a very much more deliberate beat does not take them by surprise.   The same care is necessary when the process is reversed, and a beat has to be subdivided.

In making such changes of speed as have been described, no violent or exaggerated gestures on the part of the conductor are implied ; in fact, an audience behind him need not be aware that anything is about to occur, but the players in front of him must realize a few moments previously that some change of speed is going to be made.   This " getting hold of the orchestra " is conveyed more by the eye and the attitude of the conductor than by movements of the baton, and might be described as a psychological rather than a physical effort.

An immediate change of *tempo* or of time (*b*)—the two must be clearly distinguished—that is, without any previous gradual slackening or quickening of pace, require just the same preliminary hold on the players' attention, and, perhaps, rather more than usual precision in marking the beats for the first bar or two of the new *tempo* or time.

Two things the conductor should avoid doing when making changes in the beat such as have just been described are : (1) keeping his eyes fixed on the full score, and (2) showing any hesitation in his manner of making the new beat.

(*c*) Particular emphasis or stress on a note can be expressed by a beat approached by a more extended movement of the arm, one which gives the baton greater speed in reaching its destination and, figuratively, gives the impression that one is taking a deeper breath preparatory to a greater effort.   A special emphasis or *sf.* occurring in between the beats, such as, for example, the following from Beethoven's C minor Symphony and Brahms' D major Symphony:

Ex.1.

may tempt the young conductor to make some special quick movement of the baton or hand just at the moment when the stress occurs.   In both cases it is much more important that the beat *previous* to the cross-accent should be very clearly and emphatically given, as a wholesale shifting of the accent

on to an unaccented part of the bar is apt to unsteady the
playing of the orchestra and requires some special effort in
order to counteract it.

SECTION VI

Beginning a Piece or Movement

When an orchestra makes a tentative start, when there is
hesitation or uncertainty, at the beginning of a piece or
movement (or after a pause), it is almost sure to be because
the players don't know exactly what the conductor means, or,
in other words, they are uncertain which beat of the bar he
is giving them. The only way to remove any doubts of this
sort which may prevail is to make a point of beating that
beat first which, either in whole or in part, first appears in
the score and parts. To beat blank beats which are not
shown in the score and parts is to foster uncertainty. The
amateurish "a bar for nothing" or "so many beats for
nothing" is not recommended, for two reasons : first, it is
not the universal custom ;* and, second, it may upset the
counting of empty bars in the parts by those players who are
not playing at the start. However elementary the orchestra,
there is no reason why the players should not make a good
unanimous start unless it be from lack of confidence, and
confidence need not be lacking if the players are trained to
one (the only sound) method. It is not a matter of executive
skill, but a matter of understanding and training ; and the
most elementary school orchestra should, in this respect, be
equal to the most efficient professional body.

It is essential that the players should know, before starting a piece, what the note value of the conductor's beat is
going to be ; in cases where there can be any possible doubt
—for example, when the *tempo* is such that either two or
four, two or six, one or three beats to the bar may be given—
a word from the conductor is all that is needed to remove any
uncertainty. When the players know *how many* beats in a
bar there are to be, all that they further require is to observe
which beat of the bar, either in whole or in part, in notes
or in rests, appears first in the music. The conductor being
equipped with the same knowledge, he then only need take
care that the movement of his baton which precedes and
leads up to the initial beat is given amply and deliberately
enough for the players to be able to gauge exactly when the
motion of the baton will culminate in the beat.

* It is, in fact, "not done" by professional conductors.

Many pieces begin on the first beat of a bar; the baton must move from the stationary starting position (Figs. 1, 2, 3, A), curl round, rise, and then fall to the down-beat in one continuous cumulative movement.

The large majority of pieces which do not begin on the first beat of a bar begin on the last; that may be the second, third, fourth, sixth, eighth, ninth, or twelfth, according to what are the time and *tempo* of the piece; or they may begin on some fractional part of the last beat. In either case the conductor should make his motion from the starting position deliberately and clearly, so that it culminates in a distinct and unmistakable up-beat.

In the following examples the first notes written and sounded are actually *on* the last beat:

and in the following they are on some part of the last beat:

(only in the last example—Mendelssohn—has the composer actually written the rest which in the other examples [Ex. 3] is imagined). In all the above cases the last beat of the bar must be distinctly given and amply prepared, whatever the note-value of the beat, whatever part of the beat the music starts on, and whichever beat the last one in the bar is, be it second, third, fourth, or what not.

It is only comparatively rarely that pieces or movements start on other than the first or last beats of a bar. Cases do

occur of a start made on the third beat of four-in-a-bar, but if
nearer the beginning of the bar than that, composers usually
supply rests which complete the bar, as in the following:

Ex 4.   TSCHAIKOWSKI

In such cases, although no notes occur, the rests appear in
all the orchestral parts, and the beats must be distinctly but
unobtrusively given. If such silent beats are given too emphatically, some player may easily regard them as an invitation to play !

Scherzi and other very quick pieces in duple or triple time,
for which the beat is only one-in-a-bar, frequently begin on
the half or (in triple time) the last third of the beat :

Ex.5.   Allegro(♩.= 96)   BEETHOVEN

The beat being only one-in-a-bar, the initial beat must
be at the *beginning* of the incomplete bar ; it is advisable
to make that an *up-beat*, so that those players who are only
counting silent bars at the start do not count one bar too
many, and thus go wrong in their reckoning.

The best-drilled of orchestras may bungle a start if there is
any doubt as to what note-value the conductor adopts for his
beat.   The following *Andante*, for example, from Haydn's
E flat symphony—

Ex.6.

might easily be taken at two-crotchets-in-a bar by one conductor, and at four-quavers-in-a-bar by another. The one
would begin beating at the half-bar, the other at the last
quarter. Unless the players *know* which he is going to adopt,
the first two or three notes may be badly played even by the
best of orchestras. It is the conductor's duty to make up his
own mind first, and then to make his decision known to the
orchestra.

SECTION VII

Pauses and Leads

The handling of pauses in the music by a conductor is very liable to expose any weakness in his technique and in his training of the orchestra. Uncertainty as to what he means will cause a lack of confidence amongst the players and, as often as not, different interpretations of his meaning, with, as a result, an untidy *ensemble*.

A composer's notation does not always make it quite clear how a pause should be treated; sometimes there is nothing to show whether it is intended that a pause on a note or a chord should be cut off and followed by complete silence before a re-start is made, or whether the chord should run on without break into the next. Indeed, the treatment of a pause depends so much on the notation that, when the latter is not quite clear, the conductor has to decide for himself how he is going to manage it, and, having decided, he must make it quite plain (even if verbal explanation is necessary) to the orchestra. In this way different conductors may treat the same pause in different ways, and who is to judge between them? A matter of much more importance than the differing views of conductors, however, is that there should be no misunderstanding between conductor and orchestra; that having decided what to do, the conductor should convey his intention to the players and see that they carry out his idea.

The occurrence of pauses will fall into one or other of the following categories: A pause may occur on a rest; this means complete silence. Or it may occur on a note or chord; this means that the sound is to be continued for an unmeasured period. If on a note or chord, the pause may be followed by complete silence, or it may be followed by other notes without any break in the sound. In any case, the baton must come to a standstill on the pause, and will be held stationary for the duration of the pause.

The following are examples of pauses such as occur commonly in orchestral music, and are such that there can be little doubt, and little room for difference of opinion, as to their treatment:

Ex.7.

Here the pause follows a short note and occupies a complete bar. There is no question as to the effect intended; it is simply an interruption of the regular progress of the time, and all that is left to the conductor is to decide how long the interruption is to last. After the two crotchets are played, an unassertive down-beat, held stationary, indicates the bar and holds the silent pause; no second beat is required. The baton then moves up and then down preparatory to the next down-beat, just as is done when starting a piece on the first beat of the bar.

Ex.8.   SCHUMANN
Langsam

In Example 8 the pause on the note and the silent pause are both in the same bar, and the note has to be completely cut off. One down-beat, more assertive in manner than for a silent pause, is held till the sound is to cease, and then a sharp flick of the baton marks the sudden cessation of all sound. That flick can be made sideways or upwards, but is better not made downwards in case it might be mistaken for the down-beat of the next bar. After the "cut-off," the baton is again held stationary for the duration of the silent pause.

Ex.9.   HAYDN
Adagio

In the above case the chord is held, but there is no rest between it and the next bar; yet there can be little doubt that, being the end of a rhythmic period, the chord will be cut off before resuming the time-beat of the fifth bar. One down-beat will hold the pause, then a quiet but quite distinct flick of the baton, sideways or upwards, will cut off the chord; as part of the same movement the baton can then move towards the down-beat of the next bar, thus making no distinct second pause as was done in Example 8.

The next differs from Example 9 only in that a portion (one quaver) of an incomplete bar follows the pause, also a change of time and *tempo*. The movement of the baton to end the

pause will therefore be similar to that in Example 9, but then
a distinct up-beat, indicating the half-bar of the *presto*, must

Ex.10.

be made, just as has been described in Section IV. when a piece
starts on some part of the last beat in a bar. Thus Examples 9
and 10 involve only one stationary position of the baton each,
whereas Example 8 requires two.

Ex.11.

In Example 11 the last note of a phrase, a silent pause,
and the first note of another phrase all occur in one half-bar
or (without the pause) in one beat. The baton must come to
a standstill *on* the second beat; thus, one action serves to
give the beat and to hold the silent pause; then the second or
up-beat must be given *over again* in order to mark the start for
the next phrase.

Ex.12.

Here are two pauses in one bar, the first of which is not cut
off, while the second undoubtedly is. The rhythmical structure
at this point calls for a distinct break, and this is confirmed
by two little lines inserted (presumably) by the composer to
make sure of the break. The baton will come to a standstill
on the down-beat, and then move on to the second without any
intervening flick; held stationary there, a slight flick will cut
off the sound, when, without making any further pause, the
baton will rise to the third and last beat of the bar.

Ex.13.   MENDELSSOHN
Allegro molto

Somewhat similar is Example 13. A down-beat pause, which is not cut off, is followed by an up-beat pause which is cut off.

Ex.14. Allegro di molto   MENDELSSOHN

In Example 14 it is clearly intended that the chord after the pause should follow without any sort of "cut-off." All that is necessary is down-beat held stationary, followed by the upward motion of the baton which precedes the down-beat of the next bar. No sort of flick should be introduced.

Ex.15. Allegro molto   BEETHOVEN

Here, again, it is obvious that there should be no "cut-off" after the pause; but the second beat of the bar must be given clearly in order to get the A natural played at the right moment. The baton will be stationary on the first beat, and the second beat which follows will serve the double purpose of ending the pause-chord and of re-starting the next phrase.

Ex.16.   MOZART
Andante (♪)

A pause with no "cut-off" and a continuation of the phrase all in the same beat needs some care, and a clear understanding of what the conductor is doing. The baton will halt on the second quaver-beat, then, in order to get the two hemi-demi-semi-quavers played together and in time, it will be necessary to repeat the second beat.

Something in between a complete "cut-off" and a continuous sound may be suitable in certain cases. The chords at the beginning of Mendelssohn's Midsummer Night's Dream over-ture do not call for very marked separation, and there is no rest or pause between them; yet enough break must be made to enable the wind players to separately articulate each note. The down-beat held stationary will make the pause, followed by an up-beat which moves without any break to the down-beat of the next bar; the effect is as if just enough time is allowed between the chords to, as it were, take breath; the up-beat secures the end of each chord and, at the same time, prepares for the coming down-beat.

Occasionally some instruments have to hold a pause while others are required to go on playing in time for some part of the bar. The following requires all four beats of the bar, of which the fourth is held stationary, followed by a flick to cut off the sound at the end of the bar:

It is well to make all such movements of the baton as have been described simply and clearly, without any unnecessary flourishes, which are only likely to confuse or mislead the players; also to guard against making more than one down-beat in a bar. Extra down-beats, or beats which look like down-beats, may not only be misunderstood by those who are playing, but may also be counted as bars by those who are not playing at the time.

Leads.—Theoretically, all players in an orchestra should make their "leads," or entries, quite independently of any gesture or help from the conductor, but in practice a conductor will always turn to a player, or group of players, with a help-ful invitation to make an *important* entry with confidence. If the entry is not at all a prominent feature of the music it is better to leave the players to make it unassisted, for when they are accustomed to be given every lead the players will get to depend too much on the conductor and too little on their own initiative to make confident re-entries; moreover, places are bound to occur when several parts are required to enter in close succession, and any attempt by the conductor to give each of them a sign would only result in a series of quick gestures or looks which would be more confusing than helpful.

Like all other conductor's actions, the look or gesture which invites a confident entry must be given before the actual moment when the entry is due : two or three seconds may suffice, but half a second may be too late. It is, perhaps, rather more the look than the gesture that gives players the necessary confidence to re-enter, especially after long periods of counting blank bars, and it need not appear as if they were being physically "dragged in," or threatened with dire punishment should they fail to take up their lead.

SECTION VIII

REHEARSING

EXPERIENCE has shown that it is easier to acquire, and to teach, the purely physical part of the conductor's art than it is to cultivate those qualities which make a conductor able to rehearse and train an orchestra. The embryo conductor will—or should—face the fact that his most formidable task will be, not in learning how to manipulate the baton or how to manage his own person, but in learning to recognize faults in orchestral playing, in knowing how to eliminate them, and in gaining the power which will enable him to make the playing of the orchestra under his charge technically excellent. / The physical part of conducting can be practised alone, but the other can only be acquired by experience, with the help of, and probably at the expense of, a real live orchestra.

When first taking charge of a rehearsal the beginner's most likely sensations will be those which arise from a quite natural and excusable self-consciousness. The weight of unaccustomed responsibility, coupled with the idea that everybody is watching him, are almost sure to dominate his thoughts and divert them from the playing of the music to himself. Feeling that he must assert his authority and prove his competence, the tyro may then fasten on some trivial matter as being worthy of correction, and stop the playing in order to point it out, the while he fails to notice the grossest of faults. The fact is, being embarrassed by an unfamiliar situation, he does not really hear what is going on. His thoughts are apt to be centred on what he himself is doing and on how he is doing it, instead of on what the players are doing and how they are doing it. The idea that he is *conducting* must give way to the fact that the orchestra is *playing*; the playing of the music is what an audience will be assembled to *hear*; they do not really meet to *see* the conducting of the conductor, although they may be interested to hear how a particular conductor interprets a particular piece of music.

When the elements of time-beating have been mastered, the aspiring conductor should concentrate all his faculties on *listening*, on learning to hear how the music is being played. His first duty is to *hear critically what is going on*, his second is to *know what he wants*, and his third to *know how to get it.*

The first of these is by no means so simple a matter as it may sound. The effect of an orchestra playing, when heard from the position of the conductor, is very different to the effect as it is heard by a listener some distance away : there is much more resonance at such close quarters, more jumbling up of sounds ; the instruments situated close to the conductor are heard individually in a way that they are not heard by an audience ; the effect to the ears of the latter is more thoroughly blended into one whole, as it were, more toned down. It is very true of the sound of an orchestra that " distance lends enchantment," but that does make the task of the conductor easier, because it is equally true that faulty *ensemble* will be more noticeable from some distance off than from the centre of things. Only the experience of doing it will help the beginner to hear what is going on in the orchestra from the standpoint of the conductor, and then only when his mind is not diverted from listening by the effort required to carry out the physical movements of time-beating or by any feeling of self-consciousness. In this respect it is of advantage to a conductor to have had some actual experience of orchestral playing ; the effects as they sound at close quarters are then not so unfamiliar, and can be co-related with what is heard from a greater distance ; indeed, experience as a player is from every point of view a quite valuable asset in the equipment of anyone who aspires to control the playing of others. Failing that, any opportunity that may present itself of sitting amongst or near to the instrumentalists during a rehearsal is one that should be eagerly grasped.

The knowledge of what he wants provides the standard at which the conductor aims, and the process of getting what he wants consists of eliminating all that is not good in orchestral playing. and of making the players under his direction realize in sound the effects demanded by his standard.

How thoroughly an orchestra can be rehearsed must obviously depend on the amount of time available, and on the capability of the players. In the case of amateur bodies there is usually a series of practices—perhaps a weekly meeting—for a month or more in preparation for a concert; whereas, for economic reasons, a professional orchestra is usually limited to a small or even a quite inadequate amount of time in which to prepare for a public performance. In the first case a considerable proportion of the time must be devoted to teaching the members of the orchestra to play their parts correctly, while in the second, executive efficiency may be taken for granted, and the conductor may have little else but the *ensemble* and interpretation of the music to consider.

The word "orchestra" is so all-embracing that it is quite impossible to suggest a method of rehearsing which will cover all cases; three musicians playing in a tea-shop are often called an orchestra; the word is so elastic that it does not distinguish between a trio of instrumentalists and a body of one hundred professional musicians assembled for a musical festival. For convenience, and in order to establish some sort of a standard, orchestras will in the present instance be classed in four groups, as follows:

(*a*) *School orchestras*, incompletely constituted, and endowed with only quite elementary executive powers, but blessed with frequent and regular times for practice.

(*b*) *Amateur orchestras*, more or less complete, and usually stiffened with professional help for concerts, with limited execution, but fairly numerous opportunities for rehearsing.

(*c*) *Second-class professional orchestras*, more or less complete, technically efficient, but granted few rehearsals.

(*d*) *First-class professional orchestras*, complete, technically efficient, but, under present conditions in England, often woefully under-rehearsed.

(*a*) The SCHOOL ORCHESTRA usually consists of strings, with a strong preponderance of violins, few, if any, violas, one or two violoncellos, and possibly a double-bass. It is generally necessary to supply harmonic support on a piano, and wind instruments, if there are any, are few, and their selection appears to be governed more by chance than by choice.

The duties of the conductor may include the responsibility of selecting the pieces to be played. In the case of a school orchestra this requires some careful discrimination, because ordinary standard orchestral works are usually far beyond the executive powers of the young players. A considerable and increasing quantity of music specially designed for school use is now available (mostly for string orchestra with an *ad lib.*

piano part), in which the string parts are not too difficult for
young people of two or three years' experience. These will
serve the purpose of a school orchestra more usefully and more
effectively than distorted versions of the more difficult works
designed for concert purposes. Also, the absence of wind
instruments in most schools makes it almost impossible to
present ordinary works scored for full orchestra in any but an
inartistically mangled form. Young people can hear the
classics of the concert room more efficaciously by means of the
gramophone than by mutilations of their own making. The
school orchestra, however rudimentary its standard, will be a
better musical educator for its members when the tone, *ensemble*,
and intonation are good, than when these are bad owing to
totally inadequate technique; these essentially musical qualities
are only possible of attainment when the music played lies
within the range of the players' executive ability.

The study of a few pieces, with a view to a concert performance, will most likely occupy the practices for several weeks or
even for a whole term; and with this should be mixed some
regular practice in sight-reading; a third or a quarter of the
time available is very well spent in this way, and the process
should be to play on without stopping unnecessarily to make
corrections.

It is advisable to mix the stronger and the weaker players so
that they are evenly distributed amongst the first and the
second violins, and to occasionally change over the entire side
of first violins to play second violin, and *vice versa*. By this
means the weaker members get better and more profitable
practice than if they are placed all together at the tail-end of
the second violins.

It is quite excusable, and need not dismay a beginner, should
he find that at first the faults in the playing of a school
orchestra are so many and so inextricably mixed up that he does
not quite realize what is wrong, nor where to begin putting
things right. A lot of wrong notes, wrong note-values, bad
intonation and what not, all hurled at his aural sense in one
dreadful mass, may be difficult to diagnose and difficult to cure.
Experience will gradually help the victim to segregate these
troubles, and then to deal with them one by one.

The following is suggested as the order in which faults should
be attacked : first get the *time* right (the note-values correct),
and so get the body to move roughly together ; then tackle the
wrong notes, and so reduce the tonality to some sort of order ;
after that, the worst of the faulty intonation might have some
attention. Technical difficulties in the parts will come more or
less under the heading of wrong notes (or, what is much worse

to remedy, no notes at all), and must be taken as part of the process of getting the right notes played. When these main faults have been reduced, and the piece begins to sound something like itself, the *ensemble* (unanimous movement of parts, attack, etc.) may be considered, and at this point, when the players are getting familiar with their parts, a closer connection between the movements of the conductor and the playing can be established. Finally, the light and shade, expression, and perhaps a few more delicate adjustments can be made, and by then the playing will probably be as good as it can be made. It is wasteful to spend much time on refinements and subtleties when the general standard of executive ability is low; much better, get the orchestra to play boldly, if somewhat roughly, together, to encourage confidence, and to instil into the minds of the players their duties as one each of a team.

(*b*) AMATEUR ORCHESTRAS.—These, if regularly organized permanent societies, usually practise together for some time before a concert, and consist mainly of strings, with a possible sprinkling of wind instruments. The professional element generally appears at a final rehearsal, and will more or less complete the wind department or strengthen any weak section of the strings. Their musical food will be the standard works of the concert room as far as their technical ability and financial resources will allow.

Executive ability varies considerably amongst amateur string players, but on the average it will be equal to rendering the parts in classical orchestral pieces with the aid of some individual practice when necessary for passage work or any other technical difficulty.

As in dealing with a school orchestra, the conductor will first be obliged to devote some time to familiarizing the players with their parts. Inaccuracies of notes and time must be put right, the entries made confident, and any executive difficulties must be tackled before going into the greater subtleties of interpretation and style. When the parts are becoming familiar to the player the *ensemble* will claim attention, and therein will lie, most probably, the most severe test of the conductor's thoroughness. Finish, style, and interpretation generally may be looked upon as a last stage in the process of building up such a rendering of the music as can be expected from those whose love of the art (it should be remembered) is the only reason why they devote themselves to orchestral playing.

In dealing with any sort of amateur body the conductor will probably be faced with the difficulty of overcoming a certain tentative manner of playing which may not be due to any technical difficulties in the parts, but simply to a lack of confidence. Timid, hesitating playing produces all the worst faults of the *ensemble*; the tendency to wait for the sounds of other instruments before playing engenders a bad attack, and this fault is usually accompanied by a similar tendency to trail on a little after the end of the notes. Both unite to give an "untidy" effect to the playing, and to destroy all the cleanness, the crispness, and the unanimity of movement which is the essence of a good *ensemble*.

Provided that the timidity is not due to difficulty of execution, there is no good reason why amateur playing should not be prompt in attack and unanimous in moving from note to note. Time will be well spent in taking a simple phrase (it must be quite free from technical difficulties) over and over again till every player, from the strongest to the weakest, attacks every note with confidence, and moves from one note to another with absolute precision and with the right amount of tone. A lesson of this sort leaves behind a distinct impression on the mind of the player, and can be referred to (it may not be necessary to repeat it often) whenever hesitation and untidiness again assert themselves. The same method will serve when a particular tone-gradation is not forthcoming. Once the players have been made to produce, say, a satisfactory *pianissimo*, they have demonstrated to themselves that they *can* do it; when similar situations occur again, the conductor need only recall to their minds the fact that they *have* previously done it in order to ensure the reproduction of the same effect.

Many amateurs have difficulty in counting a number of blank bars in their parts. It should be insisted that *everyone* counts their own empty bars, and that nobody relies on anyone else to do it. There are at least two unsound ways of counting, and only one reliable way. One of the unsatisfactory ways is to mentally count the *beats* of the bar over and over again, while at the same time endeavouring to keep a separate account of the complete bars; the other is to count thus:

($\frac{4}{4}$) *One*-two-three-four, *two*-two-three-four, *three*-two-three-four, and so on.

The only efficient way of doing it is to *count complete bars only*, thus:

One — — —, two — — —, three — — —, and so on

[the dashes represent the beats which are only felt, but are not mentally counted].

That the services of the players are voluntary should always be at the back of the mind of a conductor of amateur orchestras.

The individual members of such bodies are no less sensitive than professional instrumentalists, and the exercise of a certain amount of tact will often be necessary when situations arise which could hardly occur where orchestral players are paid for their services. The musical discipline need be no less severe, but the "drill-sergeant" manner is to be avoided if a conductor would hold his voluntary forces together and keep their interest alive.

(c) SECOND-CLASS PROFESSIONAL ORCHESTRAS.—By "second-class" must be understood such orchestras as are employed at theatres, the larger cinemas, sometimes in seaside towns,* and at places of amusement generally. The constitution is often rather short of being a complete concert orchestra, and the number of players to each string part may be small. The personnel, though they may have been trained in a school rather rougher than that of the first-class "symphony" player, are nevertheless technically efficient. The music they play will lean more or less to the light side, and the time available for rehearsing is sure to be reduced to a minimum quantity, if, indeed, it is not whittled down to vanishing-point. The players in these orchestras are generally good readers, and have little difficulty in playing their parts as far as execution is concerned.

The rehearsing of such orchestras, which must be economically planned so as to cover as much ground as possible, will be largely occupied in improving the *style* of the playing. A coarse quality of tone, disregard of the phrasing (as distinguished from the string bowing), the over-playing of accompanying parts, for example, are bad faults in style which may quite easily exist side by side with a prompt and "slick" manner of playing; these shortcomings may be expected in the smaller and lighter orchestras whose members may be accustomed to a style of rendering more rough-and-ready than refined.

A tendency to "race" when playing quick movements frequently exists in orchestras of this class; it is the result of playing much light music (marches, musical comedy selections) as a matter of routine, and unfortunately is often allowed to pass for brilliancy. The loss in both quantity and quality of tone is considerable when an orchestra is allowed to tear through quick movements at breakneck speed. Only a stern refusal on the part of the conductor to be "rushed" will cure an orchestra of this trying and inartistic habit. In connection with this, drummers should be particularly closely watched,

---

* These are sometimes "double-handed"; that is, the string players are all able to play wind instruments as well, so that the orchestra can be turned into a military band for use out of doors.

and checked when they take upon themselves to force the pace.

(d) First-Class Professional Orchestras.—There are not many of these in England, nor are they necessarily permanently organized bodies in which the same personnel always plays together. Even though an orchestra bears a name, the individual members may vary from year to year or even from concert to concert. The efficiency of all the players may be taken for granted, although their quality is bound to vary with the individual. Full concert orchestras usually have an adequate number of string players to each part, and all wind instruments demanded in the scores of the pieces that are to be played are provided. The ordinary rule is one rehearsal for one concert; two rehearsals may occasionally be conceded, but must be regarded as rather exceptional, while for a series of daily concerts in which a familiar repertoire is played, two or three rehearsals a week are all that can be expected. Of such players who are engaged for first-class concerts it may be said that they are familiar with all the standard works which make up the bulk of most programmes, and are in no sense reading at sight, except in the cases of new or, perhaps, rarely played pieces.

It is true that a young conductor without either reputation or much experience is not often likely to have the chance of conducting orchestras such as have just been described. The most probable case is that of a young composer who is given the opportunity of rehearsing and conducting a work of his own. This is certainly a less severe test of his competence than when a familiar piece is the medium, because there cannot be any very precise standard by which to measure the rendering of a new piece, while in the case of a well-known work the renderings of it by so many conductors and orchestras in the past cannot but serve as standards by which any performance will be measured. In any case, as the conductor who is either young, inexperienced or unknown, will probably be conscious of some lack of authority over a body of experienced players (who will quickly sense his ability to control their playing), his attitude should be tactfully adjusted to suit the situation.

By reason of the high standard of executive skill which prevails in first-class orchestras, little time need be spent in familiarizing the players with their parts; in general, the parts will be correctly played at once, and, if passages do occur which are awkward or difficult, the players can be allowed a minute or two to try them over independently, to settle on fingering, position, or whatever it is that lies at the root of the difficulty.   The *ensemble*, the balance of tone, and all that goes to make up the conductor's interpretation of the music, can claim immediate attention without going through that preliminary stage which occupies so much more time when less efficient players are being rehearsed.

Good *ensemble* may be described as the unanimity, or the precision, with which several individuals play together; it is the hall-mark of a well-trained orchestra, and a searching test of a conductor's ability.   It covers not only the unanimity with which several players begin, hold and leave a note, but also the regulation of the amount of tone, and of its quality. It embraces both the precision with which several players of the same part move together (making that part sound like one voice) and the simultaneous movement of two or more parts in harmonic combination.   Thus, a faulty *ensemble* may show itself in the playing of, say, the first violins as a body, or the fault may lie in the synchronization of the several parts of the string orchestra; to put it yet another way, one first violin may not play quite together with another first violin, or the entire body of first violins may not play quite together with the second violins.   Faulty *ensemble* is often evident in the wood-wind group when they attack chords as a body; in the *tutti* it may be looked for in a tendency of the brass group to sound just after the strings and wood-wind, owing to the rather slower speech and articulation of all wind instruments blown through a cup-shaped mouthpiece.

Indistinct beginnings, ragged endings, and blurred harmonies are the effects of bad *ensemble*, and the cause is that some of the instruments are a little behind (more rarely in front of) the rest, or that some are sounding unduly prominently.

Only careful observation on the part of the conductor, and close attention on the part of the players, will unite in producing the clear, well-regulated, well-balanced succession of sounds which is the essence of good orchestral playing.   It is not an infinity, not a variety nor great vigour of physical movement by the conductor, not a succession of varied gestures, nor any intense display of energy which will make an orchestra play together as with one purpose.   It is rather by means of a distinct authoritative beat, combined with careful training at rehearsals, that a conductor will be able to synchronize the playing in every part of the orchestra so that it moves as one body controlled by one mind.

Only too frequently can one *hear* superficially brilliant orchestral playing and *see* apparently brilliant conducting, yet at the same time one may hear the constantly blurred effect on one section of the orchestra playing as if syncopating the harmony of another section. The exhilaration produced by mere brilliance offers insufficient compensation for the clear utterance which is lost when a conductor concentrates on brilliance and neglects the *ensemble*.

By *balancing the tone* is meant getting the right amount of tone from each orchestral part. In one sense it is the business of the composer to balance his orchestration so that the parts are heard in their right proportion, and, theoretically, the conductor should not be held responsible for faulty balance. In practice, however, a certain amount of adjustment of tone-quantity must be made by the conductor, even when the orchestration is quite well balanced. The inexperienced conductor with the score in front of him may *see* the orchestration apparently quite well balanced on paper, and may take for granted that it is equally well balanced in actual sound ; careful listening to the effect at a rehearsal will often reveal the fact that certain parts are sounding too prominently, and may be overshadowing certain other parts which are actually more important in the design of the music.

Even with the best of orchestration played by the best of orchestras, attention must be given to the balance of tone in order to ensure that the music is not being presented in a distorted form. Much orchestration, by its nature, balances itself, and requires no readjustment when it is translated into sound. Upper parts, by virtue of their higher pitch, usually take sufficient prominence over inner or lower parts ; the latter, however, if of melodic importance, will often require more reinforcement of tone-quantity than is shown on paper (in the score) if they are to stand out above secondary matter of higher pitch. Accompanying matter will sometimes have to be suppressed in order to allow sufficient prominence to melodic matter, and the more complex the design of the orchestration the more necessary is it for the conductor to observe how the sounds of the various parts penetrate in the actual playing, and to make adjustments when necessary to bring about a proper balance of tone. Much can be done in this way by the left hand of the conductor without stopping the playing ; but, if necessary, a few words explaining the function of each part may be effective in clearing up obscurity which may be due to the players not realizing exactly what is the function of their own particular part at the moment.

Some readjustment of the tone-quantity in loud *tutti* is frequently necessary owing to the overwhelming weight of brass tone when the instruments are played *fortissimo* : a conductor should not be content to hear merely a large amount of sound in a loud *tutti*; it may be that the bulk of the sound is only harmonic matter which is swamping the main melodic interest of the music, and the result is a series of heavy chords with a shadow of a melody struggling for existence.

When an orchestra is being rehearsed it should never be taken for granted that the *ensemble* and the balance of tone are good; the conductor who is too conscious of the fact that he is using his hands and arms may forget to use his ears, and will let pass unnoticed faults which mar the cleanness of the playing and cause the music to be misrepresented. The pianist who plays with one hand after the other is rightly condemned; the conductor who permits bad *ensemble* merits the same criticism. The pianist who lets his left hand overwhelm the tone of his right hand is distorting the music he plays; so is the conductor who does not properly balance the tone of his orchestra.

The following are a few not unimportant features which frequently mar good orchestral playing, and which require habitual attention at rehearsals; they are common to all grades of players, from the most elementary to the most proficient.

It is always likely that an orchestra will exhaust the possibilities of a *crescendo* at too early a stage of its course, and by doing so will rob the culmination of its proper effect. Two things require attention when making a *crescendo*: first, how long it is to last; and, second, how far the increase of tone is to be carried.

The same care should be exercised in regulating the decrease of tone in a *diminuendo*.

Failure to keep the tone-gradation at one level for a more or less prolonged period is a not uncommon fault. This is especially liable to occur when the music is to be kept soft for some time. A tendency to allow *pianissimo* to become *piano* or *mezzo piano* will often have to be checked.

To hold the tone evenly for the entire duration of a long loud note requires some effort on the part of the players; they are liable to put all the force into the beginning of the note, and then to let it drop. The brass players, especially, are prone to play in this "explosive" manner.

On the other hand, a really "explosive" effect *is* required when a note is marked *forte-piano*; this should be a *sudden* drop in the tone, not a gradual decrease.

String players may easily fail to exert themselves sufficiently in playing a *tremolo*; whether produced by a reiteration of a note (bow tremolo) or by the alternation of two notes (finger tremolo), the effect is spoiled when the notes are not reiterated or repeated as quickly as possible.

* * * * *

It will be easily understood that the players in an orchestra will work all the better at a rehearsal when the work and the conditions are made as agreeable and pleasant for them as possible. A conductor naturally wishes to get the best he can out of his orchestra during the time available; he should therefore seek to enlist the interest and goodwill of those on whom he depends to carry out his wishes, without in any way sacrificing the discipline which must necessarily be maintained when one person is charged with the control of so many others.

A rehearsal can be planned and managed so as to avoid either unnecessary monotony or the feeling on the part of the players that they are being driven at high pressure. Good work and a ready response to his efforts can hardly be expected of the players when a conductor is seemingly disinterested or lethargic; on the other hand, when artistic enthusiasm manifests itself in the form of fussiness, the effect on the players will be rather to irritate them than to interest them. To stop the playing frequently and constantly is a sure way of wearing down the patience of an orchestra; impatience breeds only annoyance, and a consequent loss of responsive effort. Mere mistakes on the part of a player can generally be corrected without stopping the playing, by a word, a glance, or if very glaring, without sign of any sort, as a player will usually be quite conscious of what is obviously wrong. Collective mistakes too, especially if self-evident, need not necessarily entail an immediate interruption of the playing; they may wait till it has to be stopped in order to draw attention to other features which may have accumulated during the playing of some portion of the music. One stoppage, in order to draw attention to several points, is more economical of time (and less trying to the orchestra) than a separate stoppage for every detail on which the conductor wishes to make some comment.

When a difficulty in one part only, or in any one section of the orchestra, demands the frequent repetition of some particular passage, it is unnecessarily wasteful of energy to insist on the whole orchestra playing it over and over again. It may be worth while, for example, to let the wind players rest while the strings are being drilled in some particular feature with which the former are not concerned, and *vice versa*; also, by so doing, the conductor may be enabled to hear all the better how the parts in question are being played.

SECTION IX

THE SCORE AND PARTS

AN amateur, while glancing at the many staves of a full score, was once heard by the writer to express his great admiration for the musicianship of anyone who could *read* that score while conducting a performance of the piece, assuming that that was what conductors had to do. By "reading a score" is meant: mentally realizing the melodic outlines, the harmonic combinations, the various shades of tone-colour produced by the instruments, and combining them in imagination as a whole; it may also involve reading by means of four different clefs, and making several transpositions. An experienced conductor who is also a good musician can read a straightforward classical full score roughly at about the rate at which it would be played, and even then many of the parts would be taken for granted as "read." The reading of the score, however, would fully occupy his attention, and would allow no time to think about and observe how it was being played. If a conductor were really reading a more complex modern score while conducting it, he would soon be left far behind by the orchestra playing the piece. The function of a conductor is primarily to control the playing of an orchestra, and this takes up *all* his attention; there is no spare time to give to deciphering a score.

It is true, professional conductors are sometimes obliged by force of circumstances to conduct unfamiliar pieces; they may even have to take an orchestra at a rehearsal through a work which they have never seen before. In either case they do not *read* that score in the ordinary sense of the word; they are merely taking the orchestra over ground which is more or less strange to them, and of which they can only get the barest of outlines in their minds before the music is, or as it is, translated into sound.

Any reading of a score that has to be done should be done before the conducting begins. The music, and a definite conception of how it is to be rendered, should be complete in the conductor's mind before he begins to rehearse a piece. Under ordinary circumstances the full score on the desk serves only as a reminder of what is coming, and may get only a hasty glance once or twice in a page; the conductor's mind is occupied with what the players are doing, with what he wants them to do, and with how he can get them to do it, and should not be distracted by the complicated mental process of reading the score. When a piece is being rehearsed the conductor needs to concentrate his faculties on listening to the playing; if he is learning to know the piece while the orchestra is learning to play it, a lot of valuable time, which might be devoted to training the orchestra, is being lost.

The glance occasionally given to the score while conducting should be comprehensive enough to cover the whole page, so as to take in its main features; if, as beginners are apt to do, a single stave—perhaps the first violin part—is closely followed with the idea of not "losing one's place," the main features of the orchestration may be missed, or they may only be grasped by the conductor when he hears them, instead of being already in his mind when they are approaching. The conductor must mentally anticipate the design of the orchestration if he is to be any use as a guide to the people who are to play it; thus, the full score in conducting should serve as a general reminder of what is coming rather than as a detailed record of what is occurring at the moment.

The engraving of full scores varies very much in the way the staves are braced together, and it may sometimes be difficult to identify at a glance the part of a particular instrument on a page containing a large number of staves. It is of some assistance to the eye if the three main groups of instrumental parts—wood-wind, brass, and strings—are each visually grouped together by means of large braces (brackets). When these are not engraved it is worth while supplying them in pencil; by this means particular parts may be more quickly located and identified.

Again, for economic reasons, certain staves may be omitted altogether from a page when, for the moment, there is no part in the music for the instruments they represent; the reduction of the number of staves on a page may thus be carried to such an extent that more than one set of staves (that is, more than one "line" of the music) may be printed on the same page. When this occurs suddenly, as it will when a fresh page is turned over, the conductor may easily lose his "whereabouts" owing to the fact that the instrumental staves are not in their usual position on the page. A mark of some sort placed between the sets of staves will help the conductor to realize where the division into sets of staves lies, and which, in the printed copy, is not always easily seen at the first glance.

It may also be helpful to mark with pencil certain important features in full scores with a view to making them prominent to the eye, such as the name of an instrument, a *rall.* or *accel.*, some change of beat or of *tempo*, or indeed any important feature which is not sufficiently prominent on the printed page; yet, on the whole, too many marks or signs on a page will only defeat their own object, because they necessarily cease to be prominent when a page is covered with marks. Incidentally, a score peppered with conductor's marks can be a source of great annoyance and trouble to subsequent users of the same score. The marking off of rhythmical periods may be especially helpful in the case of short bars combined with a rapid *tempo* such as occurs in *Scherzi* or quick waltz times.

In certain cases it may be well worth while that a conductor should devote some time to examining the orchestral parts before using them, all with a view to saving unnecessary waste of time at rehearsals, time which is most profitably given to the actual training of an orchestra Older editions of classical works are not always provided with letters or numbers placed at convenient places for the purpose of identifying particular bars from which a re-start may be made after the playing has been stopped in order to make some observation or correction. Quite a lot of time can be wasted in trying to identify a particular bar when there are no letters or numbers to refer to. If these are missing it is well worth while putting them in before using the parts at a rehearsal.

The mixing up of different editions, or even of different versions of the same piece in one set of parts, is by no means unheard of. This, again, may cause great waste of time at a rehearsal, time which might have been saved had a few moments been given to seeing that the parts correspond in essentials. Songs from operas or oratorios are frequently transposed in order to suit different voices, and it can, and does, happen that orchestral parts of the same song, but in different keys, are issued together to an orchestra. It is also as well to make sure of the key in which a vocalist intends to sing a song if there is the least likelihood of its being used in more than one key. A vocal solo may be sung to words in one language while those appearing in the score may be in another, and some adjustments to make the notes suit the syllables may be necessary. These and similar situations which can arise are almost sure to occupy time which is usually none too plentiful at rehearsals, and which, if discovered and adjusted beforehand, would amply repay the time spent on them. Lucky is the conductor whose librarian can be trusted to discover such discrepancies in score and parts before an orchestra is assembled.

Manuscript parts of a new work, if used as they come direct from the copyist, are sure to be well besprinkled with errors, and it is no exaggeration to say that half of the time available for the rehearsal of a new work can easily be taken up in putting right mistakes in the parts. A bar too many or a missing bar in a part may require several minutes to locate and correct. A conductor is not asking too much of a composer if he request that the parts of a work which have not been used before should be carefully looked over and corrected before being handed out to an orchestra. After all, it is mainly the composer's loss if his work is not properly presented, and he should realize that time occupied in correcting errors in the parts during rehearsal will probably only mean that so much less time will be available for rehearsing the music.

Light music, such as dances, operatic selections, light suites and kindred pieces, are more often than not published only in orchestral parts and not in full score. The conductor will then have to make do with one of the following : a piano " arrangement " which gives no hints as to how the work is orchestrated ; a first violin part with, possibly, a few essential " cues " or other hints ; or a " conductor's part," which is usually a condensed version of the music on two or three staves, provided with indications of the orchestration. Orchestral parts of light pieces may be more or less amply provided with so-called "cues" (additional parts engraved in small notes), by means of which one instrument is enabled to play some essential part belonging to another instrument which may not be present in a small or reduced orchestra.

SECTION X

Concertos, Solos, and Recitative

WHEN conducting a purely orchestral piece, the conductor is the sole interpreter of the music and the orchestra is his instrument. The interpretation of a concerto or other instrumental or vocal solo with orchestra is largely in the hands of the soloist; the conductor may co-operate with a soloist as joint-interpreter of a piece if the share of the orchestra is such as to require it, or he may have to act merely as an accompanist. How far the conductor shares the interpretation with the soloist depends on the nature of the music. A performance of a piano concerto by, say, Beethoven or Brahms demands that the conductor should *join* the soloist in giving adequate expression to the music ; whereas in the case of, say, a violin concerto by Paganini, the conductor sinks to the position of accompanist pure and simple. Vocal works with orchestra may be such that the vocalist is the sole interpreter, and the orchestra merely an accompanying instrument ; an aria from some nineteenth-century Italian opera will usually serve as an example of this.   On the other hand, in a vocal excerpt from Wagner's " Ring des Nibelungen," for example, the position of the vocalist is far from being that of sole interpreter ; in fact, the design of the music may be such that its main essence is expressed in the orchestral more than in the vocal part, and the actual interpretation, therefore, is rather more the work of the conductor than that of the vocalist.

In either case, however, the conductor has not the same free hand that he has when directing the performance of a purely orchestral work, and that very lack of freedom will be found to test his technique more severely than when he has sole control over the rendering of the music.

What has been said in Section IX. regarding the conductor's occasional glance at the full score in front of him does *not* apply when a soloist is playing or singing with an orchestra. A very much closer watch on the score must be kept (even though the piece is familiar to the conductor and well known to the orchestra), for no two soloists can be depended upon to render the solo part in exactly the same way.

The solo parts of piano concertos are often the most difficult to follow owing to the frequent occurrence of passage-work containing a large number of notes, and also on account of the elaborate ornamentation of the passages.   These are sometimes so involved (especially in more modern works) as to be difficult to decipher visually, and in actual perform-ance may be difficult to hear owing to the resonance of the instrument, which is sure to be placed close to the con-ductor.   Liberties with the regularity of the time-beat may also be expected, and these have to be conveyed in turn to the orchestra, between whom and the soloist the conductor acts as a go-between.   Bringing in the orchestra at the end of a long scale-passage (sometimes unevenly divided), or at the end of a trill of indefinite duration, are also difficulties which can easily take an unwatchful conductor unawares, and are best overcome by arriving at a definite understanding with the soloist as to how they are to be played.   It is next to impossible to bring in the orchestra promptly at the close of a long trill, such as frequently occurs at the end of a cadenza, unless the solo player makes a distinct " pull up " or *rallentando* at the final turn.

In a violin concerto the single line of the solo part is rather easier to grasp, but it is liable to the same liberties being taken with the regular succession of the time-beats.   A certain amount of *rubato* may always be expected in all solo playing, for which the conductor must be ever watchful and ready to communicate to the orchestra. In doing this it is advisable never to let the baton come to a complete standstill.

If a conductor requires to be on the alert for the unexpected when conducting instrumental solo pieces, he must be doubly watchful when a singer is the soloist. Music in modern style is usually of a texture in which the vocal part is more or less interwoven with the orchestral parts in a manner which does not allow the vocalist to take much liberty with the time; operatic arias of an earlier period, however, are still much used for concert purposes, and are usually so constructed that the vocal part is entirely melodic and the orchestral part a mere accompaniment. Singers of these arias (who are frequently endowed with a special gift for disturbing the time at unexpected moments) must be closely watched if the conductor is not to be surprised by some sudden "hold up" of the beat or any other vagary which cannot always be anticipated. Some extra strain will always be imposed on the conductor when a solo piece is being played, and this strain is not eased by the thought that if any mishap does occur it is not the soloist who will generally be held responsible for it!

The singing of *recitative* is so bound by tradition that it is almost essential that a conductor should have some knowledge of the subject before undertaking the task of conducting this particular style of music. When the *recitative* is accompanied by short chords, the conductor should mark the silent beats unobtrusively, but distinctly, so that they cannot be misunderstood. The beats on which the chords fall should be made much more assertively, and with ample preparatory movement of the baton. It is important to keep the down-beat which marks the beginning of each bar especially distinct, so that the players may follow the bars correctly, and to take care not to make more than one down-beat in each bar. When the accompaniment is sustained, the down-beat should be distinct, even though the harmony does not change at the beginning of a bar; the other beats can be given very lightly, or may even be ignored altogether unless some harmonic change occurs, when the beat in question must be clearly given. Any unnecessary elaboration of beat is only likely to confuse the players and disturb their confidence.

SECTION XI

Miscellaneous

The Orchestra on the Platform.—While it would be unwise to attempt to lay down rules as to the arrangement of an orchestra on a platform,* there are some maxims which, being based, as they are, on common sense, can be regarded as indisputable:

It is better to have the players of the same string part arranged in block formation rather than spread out in a long thin line.

All desks should be placed so that the players can see the conductor without having to turn their eyes or heads sideways.

The conductor should stand high enough to be seen by the players over the top of their music-desks. If he stands *too* high, the players near him will find it difficult to see the baton-movements without a certain amount of discomfort. As the leaders of the string parts are more or less close to the conductor, it is important that they should see his actions without difficulty or discomfort.

*   *   *   *   *

Customs.—A few customs which prevail in orchestras may not be known to those who have never played in them:

The string players are always seated two at a desk; of those who sit looking *across* the platform (as first and second violins generally do) the outside player—*i.e.,* the one nearest the audience—is regarded as number one. When the players face the conductor and the audience, the one on the right (that is, the conductor's left) is usually regarded as number one. When the string parts are subdivided, as they frequently are, player number one takes the upper of the two parts, and player number two the lower. Subdivisions into three or more parts are best arranged by the conductor according to circumstances which will largely depend on how many players there are to each part.

Player number two turns over the pages of the part.

*   *   *   *   *

Conductors-to-be are reminded that two pitches are used in this country. The low pitch is almost universal in concert

* This depends so much on the size and shape of the platform, and on conductors' personal opinions.

orchestras, while the old high pitch still prevails in military bands.*   As the wind players in orchestras may sometimes be imported from military bands, it is as well always to specify the pitch when engaging players.

Great trouble and annoyance may be saved by making sure before a rehearsal that any piano or organ to be used in conjunction with an orchestra is of the same pitch.

String players can alter the pitch of their instruments, although they may not like doing so.

Wood-wind players require a different instrument for each pitch.

Brass players *can* change their pitch by means of an extra slide or shank, but a separate instrument, built to suit each pitch, is preferable.

* In December, 1928, it was announced that low pitch was to be adopted by British Army bands.

PART II
THE INSTRUMENTS OF THE ORCHESTRA

SECTION I

The Constitution of the Orchestra

The orchestra is a combination of three main groups or choirs of instruments, each group melodically and harmonically self-contained; these groups are: (a) the bowed stringed instruments, (b) the wood-wind, and (c) the brass instruments. Representatives of two other types are also permanent members of the organization—namely, the percussion or drums, and the harp.

The string orchestra is organized in four parts: first violins, second violins, violas, violoncellos and double-basses, the last two of which normally play the lowest part in octaves. Violoncellos, however, may act as tenor or melodic instruments, in which case the number of independent parts may be five. Further, by dividing the members of all or any of these five parts into two, three, or more subdivisions, a number of smaller groups can be created, or, if carried to extremes, a number of independent string parts can be made which is equal to the number of players in the string orchestra.

Large orchestras may have as many as from sixteen to twenty first violins, the same number of second violins, from eight to twelve violas, eight to twelve 'cellos and eight to ten double-basses, while in smaller bodies the number of players to each part will, or should, be about in the same proportion.

The wood-wind group is organized in four pairs: two flutes, two oboes, two clarinets, and two bassoons; that is, in the symphony or concert orchestra of Beethoven's time. For use in opera, and since the first quarter of last century, the number of wood-wind instruments used for all purposes has been increased by at least one additional representative of each type, differing mainly in size, and therefore in pitch, from the normal instrument. Thus, the flutes may be joined by a piccolo; a cor anglais may be additional to the two oboes; to the clarinets and bassoons may be added larger instruments of similar type—namely, the bass clarinet and the double-bassoon. In smaller orchestras economy may require these additional instruments to be played by the second player of each pair.

45

Still more ambitious scores have frequently demanded four of each type of wood-wind instrument, or the introduction of some of the less common sizes, for example, the bass flute, the oboe d'amore, or the high E flat clarinet.

The brass group consists of three small choirs of instruments: four horns, two or three trumpets, three trombones and a tuba. These choirs also are subject to increase in size by the addition of more of the same instruments or (less commonly) by the introduction of other varieties of brass instrument, such as the bass trumpet, the contra-bass trombone, or various sizes of the tuba or saxhorn families. In French orchestras two cornets are frequently used in addition to the pair of trumpets; or when circumstances demand it, cornets are used in place of trumpets.

In addition to the two or three ordinary orchestral drums (timpani), certain other percussion instruments frequently figure in orchestras of all sorts; the most common are the bass drum, cymbals, side-drum, and triangle. Other instruments of infinite variety are used in orchestras from time to time, in accordance with the demands of the scores to be played, without, however, taking any permanent place or important part in the organization: such as the saxophones, the celesta, xylophone, bells, gongs, and imitative instruments of all sorts, are what one might call the temporary guests of the orchestra; they come and go, but the nucleus remains substantially as it has been since about the middle of last century:

Strings.	Wood-Wind.	Brass.
1st violins	2 flutes (piccolo)	4 horns
2nd violins	2 oboes (cor anglais)	2 (3) trumpets
Violas	2 clarinets (bass clarinet)	
{'Cellos	2 bassoons (double-bas-	3 trombones and
{Double-basses	soon)	tuba
	Drums	Harps

The orchestra for light opera is similarly but more economically organized. A usual combination is as follows:

1st violins (6), 2nd violins (4), violas (2), 'cellos (2), basses (2)					16
2 flutes, 1 oboe, 2 clarinets, 1 or 2 bassoons		...		...	7
2 horns, 2 cornets, 2 trombones, drums ...		...		...	7
Total	...	...	...	...	... 30

SECTION II

STRING TECHNIQUE

VIOLIN.—The technique of bowed string instruments is based on the fact that the shorter the sounding-length of a string, the higher is the pitch of the note it will sound.   The sounding-length of a string is that part of its length which is stretched between the bridge and the nut, the nut being a ridge which keeps the strings raised just above the finger-board.

The string may be temporarily shortened by pressing it down on to the finger-board with the finger; this is called "stopping" a string.   The sounding-length of a stopped string is that part which lies between the finger and the bridge.

On a violin the four strings are tuned and numbered as follows:

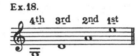

Ex.18.

4th   3rd   2nd   1st

[A string which is not stopped is said to be an *open* string.]

The first three fingers* of the left hand can, by shortening the sounding-lengths of the strings, supply the diatonic notes

FIG. 4.

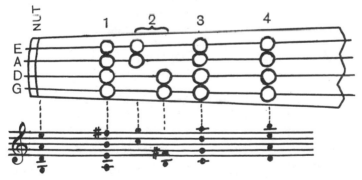

FINGERS STOPPING THE STRINGS

* In string fingering the first is the index finger, the second is the middle finger, and so on.

which lie between the fifths of the open strings, and the fourth finger can so far shorten a string that it will sound the same note as the next open string above it. The diagram, Fig. 4, p. 47, shows the positions of the fingers on the strings when placed to play in the key of G major; below are the notes that will be sounded.

Without moving the hand from its position, any finger can be placed a little further back or further forward so as to either lower or raise the diatonic notes by a semitone. Thus, whenever a semitone occurs in a scale the two fingers concerned will be placed close together, whereas for a whole tone they must lie so far apart as to leave a gap corresponding in distance to a semitone in pitch.

A chromatic scale involves the use of the same finger twice in succession, thus:

FIG. 5.

FINGERS ON G STRING

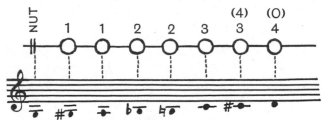

[Alternative fingerings for C sharp and D are shown in brackets.]

The same fingering on the D string will obviously sound a fifth higher, thus continuing the succession of semitones upwards.

Extension of the upward compass, and many alternative ways of fingering, are provided by moving the hand up the neck of the violin, towards the bridge, in stages which are called *positions*. The first position is that shown in Fig. 4. If moved up the neck so far that the first finger is where the second was, and the other fingers each one note higher, the hand is in the second position (see Fig. 6).

Another stage higher, with the first finger where the second was in the second position, or where the third finger was in the first position, will put the hand in the third position. In the same way the hand can be shifted higher and higher in successive positions till the end of the finger-board is reached.

As the sounding-length of the string gets shorter, the

relative distances between the fingers also require to be shortened, till in the higher positions a tone is made with the fingers as close together as would only make a semitone in the first position.   That, and the fact that the strings are further and further away from the finger-board as it approaches the bridge, contribute to make playing in the higher positions more difficult than in lower; thus, the upward compass of the violin depends on the skill of the player.   Good orchestral players of the present day will hardly be disconcerted if asked to ascend to the eleventh and twelfth positions.   For ordinary orchestral purposes the ninth position may be considered a reasonable

FIG. 6.

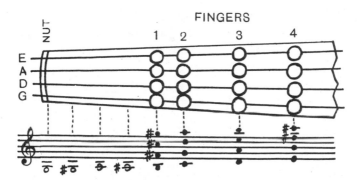

upward limit,* giving as its highest note on the E string the C which is three octaves above middle C, and played with the fourth finger.   According to the class of player, the demands on the higher positions on the violin must gradually fall till, in dealing with, say, the members of a school orchestra, it will be unwise to expect anything above the third position.

Harmonics.—If a string is touched lightly (that is, not pressed down on to the finger-board) at certain points it will, when sounded by the bow, vibrate in parts.   A string can be made to vibrate in halves by touching it at the point midway between the nut and the bridge; the note sounded will then be an octave higher than the open string.   Similarly, by touching the string at points which are, respectively, at a third and a quarter of its length, the notes sounded will be a twelfth and two octaves higher than the open string.   Notes so produced are called *natural harmonics*, and are of lighter quality than that of notes produced by full-length vibrations.

* Beethoven never wrote higher than A for the violin.

The following are—(*a*) the natural harmonics available without any technical difficulty on the four strings of the violin, and (*b*) the usual notation for these harmonics :

The octave harmonic is indicated by an O over the note, the twelfth and double octave by diamond-headed notes placed at the spot *where the string is touched by the finger*.

A string *stopped* by the first finger and *touched* by the fourth finger at a quarter of its sounding-length will sound two octaves higher than the stopped note, thus :

In the above example the lowest note is B, stopped by the first finger in the first position on the A string; the diamond-headed note shows where the string is touched (at E) by the fourth finger (and the two together form the usual notation); the high B in brackets is the sound of the harmonic which will be produced. These are called *artificial harmonics*, and are practicable on any note up to the third or fourth positions, or even higher, but should not be expected in quick succession.

Double-Stopping.*—As the bow can sound any two adjacent strings at the same moment, it follows that any two notes which can be fingered at the same time on adjacent strings can be played together. This is called double-stopping; even though one of the notes is an open string and, therefore, strictly speaking, is not stopped, the same term is used. Double-stopping is possible on any part of the finger-board, but the higher the position of the hand, the more difficult and impracticable does it become. For orchestral purposes double-stops are not usually demanded in any position higher than the third; that position will therefore be taken as the upward limit in the following explanation. Any open string

* For fuller explanation see Carse, *Practical Hints on Orchestration* (Augener), chapter iii.

and any note which can be stopped on the string either above
or below it will make an easy double-stop; thus, the open D
string can be played at the same time with any note playable
on the G string, and also with any note playable on the A
string.   The following series is therefore available:

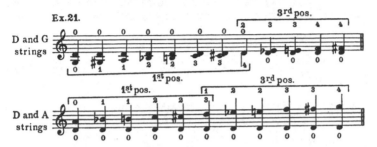

The same notes transposed a fifth higher are obviously
equally practicable on the D and A, and on the A and E
strings.

All other intervals within the octave are playable by stopping two adjacent strings at the same time.   Taking the third
position as an upward limit, the following shows the compass
for all intervals and their enharmonics:

The above include, of course, many double-stops in which
open strings are employed.

Although all the above are possible, some of them are much
easier to play than others.   Generally speaking, those re-
quiring the hand to be in the second position are the most
awkward to pitch on.   As it is always more effective to employ
an easy double-stop in preference to one which is awkward,
a good all-round rule for non-players is: use the *larger*
intervals—namely, octaves, sevenths, sixths, and fifths—in
preference to their inversions, the unison, seconds, thirds, and
fourths.

Three-note chords (triple-stops) can be played on a violin almost simultaneously (always provided each note is on a different string), although only two notes can be sustained, these being the upper two. Thus, three-note chords are generally used to give power when the chords are short and loud. The following forms of common chords, dominant sevenths, and diminished sevenths are the most practicable:

Ex. 23.

A few four-note chords are available, the best being major and minor common chords in the following positions:

Ex. 24.

Bowing.—When two or more notes are played in the same bow they follow one another without any break in the continuity of the sound, or, in other words, they sound absolutely *legato.* The notes played in the same bow are covered by a slur, which in string music is used only to show the bowing, but not the phrasing. If unslurred, each note will be given a separate bow, normally *down* (⊓, from heel to point) and *up* (V, from point to heel) alternately; the effect is that each note is separately articulated, although they are not necessarily completely detached one from the other. Many varieties of bowing are used by violinists, of which the following are common; the difference in the effect must be heard before it can be appreciated:

Ex. 25.

Slurred **legato**.............................

Legato with separate bows.................

Staccato, each note articulated and short.

Each note articulated, but long.................

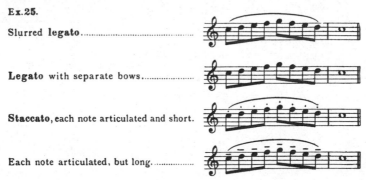

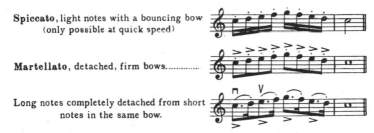

Spiccato, light notes with a bouncing bow (only possible at quick speed)

Martellato, detached, firm bows..............

Long notes completely detached from short notes in the same bow.

Tremolo.—A violinist can reiterate the same note (or a double-stop) at almost unlimited speed; this is called *bow-tremolo*, and must be distinguished from the measured repetition of the same note.   By alternating two notes *on the same string* during the progress of the same bow, another effect, called *finger-tremolo*, is produced.   The two notes of a finger-tremolo should not be more than a fourth apart:

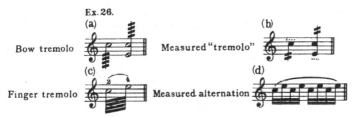

Ex. 26.

(a) Bow tremolo   (b) Measured "tremolo"

(c) Finger tremolo   (d) Measured alternation

Of the above only (*a*) and (*c*) are real tremolo effects; the notes are repeated (or alternated) at such a rate that they could not be counted; (*b*) and (*d*) are played so that each note (semi-quavers in the above examples) is given its correct value; the effect is very different from the real tremolo.

Other String Effects.—Varieties in the tone-colour of violins and bowed string instruments generally are produced by—

(*a*) *Pizzicato*—plucking the string with the finger.   The contradiction is *arco*.

(*b*) *Con sordini*—placing a mute on the bridge.   The contradiction is *senza sordini.*

(*c*) *Sul ponticello*—playing with the bow near the bridge.

(*d*) *Sul tasto*—playing with the bow on or near the finger-board.

(*e*) *Sul G, D, A, or E*—playing on the G or any other specified string.

(*f*) *Col legno*—playing with the stick of the bow.   The bow is *thrown* on the string and rebounds, therefore the sound cannot be sustained.

VIOLA.—From the point of view of technique the viola is a

large violin pitched a perfect fifth lower. The four strings
are :

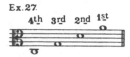

Ex.27.
4th 3rd 2nd 1st

The notation is in the alto clef, but when more convenient
for higher passages, the treble clef is used.

The technique is identical with that of the violin, but the
larger stretch between the fingers on the finger-board renders it
a little less facile, and the notes " speak " a little less readily.
For orchestral purposes the upward compass may be said to
extend to round about the C three octaves higher than the sound
of the lowest string ; this may be increased or reduced in range
according to the ability and class of the individual player.   In
finger-tremolo the interval should not exceed a perfect
fourth.

'CELLO.—The four strings are pitched an octave below those
of the viola :

Ex.28.
4th 3rd 2nd 1st

Notation is in the bass, tenor, or treble clef, according
to convenience.   Formerly, when the treble clef was used, the
notes were written an octave higher than the real sounds, and
some uncertainty still exists as to the use of the treble clef for
'cello music.   In modern music the notes are usually written at
the real pitch, but in many older scores it will be found that
when the treble follows the tenor clef, the notes are written as
they sound, whereas when the treble follows the bass clef the
notes are written an octave too high.   There is no sensible
reason why all notes should not be written as they sound.

The fingering of the 'cello in the lower positions differs from
that of the violin and viola owing to the greater distance on the
finger-board between the notes.   While semitones can be made
with adjacent fingers, a tone cannot be made with either the
second-third or with third-fourth fingers; thus, a tone above
a note which is stopped by the second finger must be stopped
by the fourth finger.   Above the fourth position the fingering
is like that of the violin.   In the highest positions the thumb is
brought on to the finger-board.

A range of three octaves above the lowest string is an
approximate compass for orchestral use, but, as with all other

string instruments, it is impossible to lay down a definite upward limit.

Of the double-stops which are feasible on the 'cello, the perfect fifths, major and minor sixths, are the best, and in that they are all possible (while certain other intervals are either awkward or impossible), it will be a sound rule for non-players on the instrument if they avoid writing other than these intervals.

Other features of violin technique—the bowing, harmonics, *tremolo, pizzicato,* etc.—are similar on the 'cello, but the shorter bow of the latter should be borne in mind in connection with slurring.   The interval between the two notes of a finger-tremolo should not exceed a major third.

DOUBLE-BASS.—The four-stringed instrument now generally used in orchestras is tuned as follows :

Ex. 29.

The above are the written notes ; the actual pitch of a double-bass part is always an octave below the notation ; the latter is normally in the bass clef except for very high notes, when the tenor clef may be used.

A compass of rather over two octaves need hardly ever be exceeded for ordinary orchestral purposes.

The fingering in the lower positions is first-fourth to make a tone, while first-second or second-fourth, will make semitones. 'Cello fingering is used in the higher positions.

Double-stopping is possible within rather confined limits, but is neither very effective nor very common.

Some natural harmonics are good, but for ordinary purposes artificial harmonics cannot be considered practicable.

The shortness of the bow should be remembered when the parts are bowed.   Bow-tremolo is both practicable and effective, while finger-tremolo is less effective and, indeed, often hardly possible, owing to the great distance between the notes on the finger-board in the lower positions.

Pizzicato, it need hardly be said, is very effective, and is very commonly employed.

SECTION III

Wind Instruments : Practical Acoustics

On all wind instruments sound is produced by causing the column of air in a tube to vibrate; this condition is brought about, *not by blowing air through the tube*, but by agitating or exciting the air at one end of the column into a state of vibration. It is done either by sending a current of air *across* an opening at one end of the tube, or by means of semi-flexible artificial reeds (thin cane), or by the lips of the player acting as reeds. Whatever the means of generating the vibrations, the column of air vibrates either in whole or in parts, and can be made to produce sounds the pitch of which depends on (*a*) the length of the tube, and (*b*) the rate of the vibrations.

The fundamental note of any particular length of tube is the lowest sound that it can be made to produce, and the relations between the length of the tube, the pitch of its fundamental note, and the rate of vibration required to sound that note, are definitely fixed by nature, and are unalterable.

A tube of approximately 2 feet in length * will sound middle C (on the piano) as its fundamental note ; the C an octave lower requires 4 feet of tube ; yet an octave lower requires 8 feet, and so on. Thus the various notes C and their corresponding lengths of tube in feet are as follows :

It will be observed that a note an octave lower than any given note requires double the length of tube. The same relative proportions apply to all intermediate notes, which, roughly calculated, are as follows for the octave between 8′ and 4′ C :

For the next octave above, these figures only require to be divided by two, and by four for the octave above that

* Only approximate measurements are given here ; the exact measurements are only scientifically interesting.

again. Similarly, for the lower octave (8′ C to 16′ C) the figures are multiplied by two.

The following shows the approximate lengths of the tubes of the ordinary orchestral wind instruments of the present day:

FIG. 7.

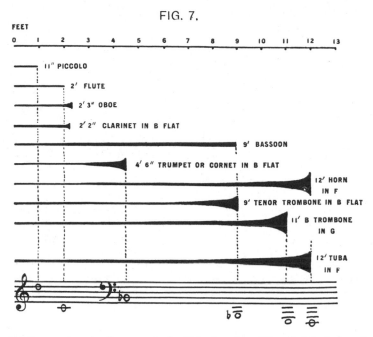

[Instruments actually measured will be found to differ slightly in length from the above, because (a) the necessary length for a given pitch is influenced in some small degree by the diameter of the bore, (b) the sounding-length only is given. For example, a flute sounds only from the mouth-hole (where the vibrations are generated) to the foot-end, and there are about 2½ inches more of tube beyond the mouth-hole; thus, a flute will be found to have a total length of about 26½ inches : on the other hand, the vibrations in the oboe are generated at the extreme end, where the reed is, so that the total length of the instrument, including the reed, is its sounding-length.]

Having grasped the relation between the length of a tube and the pitch of its fundamental sound, the next step concerns the other notes which can be sounded on the same tube by means of an increased rate of vibration. These notes are produced by increased pressure exercised by the lips of the player, who forces the air current through a more compressed opening, or in a thinner stream, which, in effect, means denser and, therefore, quicker vibrations. The following shows the series of sounds obtainable on the same tube by increased pressure; this is nature's series of harmonics, and those given in the example are for tubes of (a) 8-feet, (b) 9-feet, and (c) the first four notes of a 2-foot tube:

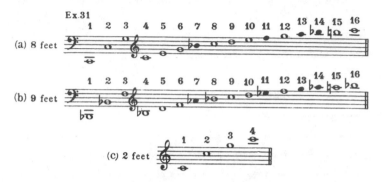

[The black notes are not quite in tune with the tempered scale.]

It will be observed that (a) is only the same series of notes as (b), but a tone higher. A similar series is obtainable on any length of tube, the intervals of which will always bear exactly the same relation to the fundamental note, and will differ only in pitch according to the length of the tube. This series of notes should be committed to memory by anyone who would understand wind instruments.

It has been stated that a similar series is obtainable on any length of tube. That is, however, in theory only, but not in practice. This leads to an important axiom which, in its turn, demonstrates the first essential difference between wood-wind and brass instruments—namely: a tube with a wide bore (inside diameter) in proportion to its length sounds its fundamental note and the next two or three harmonics easily, but can only be made to sound the higher harmonics either with difficulty or not at all; whereas, on a tube with a narrow bore in proportion to its length, the fundamental note is either difficult or impossible to produce, but the rest of the series are more or less easily sounded, in some cases even up to the sixteenth. *Wood-wind instruments are made with a wide bore in proportion to their length, and therefore use only the first few notes of the series* (Example 31, c); *brass instruments are made with a narrow bore in proportion to their length, and therefore use the higher notes of the series—namely, those numbered 2 to 8, or, in extreme cases, those numbered 2 to 16.*

For the sake of clearness the whole series will be called

harmonics, and will be distinguished by their number, the fundamental being counted as No. 1. (See Example 31, *a* and *b*.)

The bore of only a few wind instruments is strictly conical; most of them, especially the brass group, have partially cylindrical bores, but in spite of that, all except the clarinet family sound their harmonics in the order given in Example 31. The clarinets have this peculiar property (owing, it is said, to their cylindrical bore and the fact that one end of the tube is virtually closed), that they sound only alternate harmonics—namely, Nos. 1, 3, and 5. Also, the length of tube required to sound any given note on a stopped tube (*i.e.*, closed at one end) is half as much as that which is necessary to sound the same note on a tube open at both ends.

The axiom given above when applied to some actual instrument works out as follows:

Instrument.	Length.	Bore.	Harmonics mostly in use.	Proportions.
Flute	24 ins.	$\frac{3}{4}$ in.	Nos. 1 to 4	} Wide bore—short
Clarinet (B flat)	26 ins.	$\frac{1}{2}$ in.	Nos. 1 and 3	} length
Trumpet (B flat)	4 ft. 6 ins.	$\frac{1}{2}$ in.	Nos. 2 to 8	Narrow bore—greater length
Horn (F) ...	12 ft.	$\frac{1}{2}$ in.	Nos. 2 to 12	Narrow bore — still greater length

[Here, again, only rough measurements are given; these are near enough to the actual measurements to enable the reader to understand the relation between length of tube and width of bore as far as it affects the production of the harmonic series. With regard to the brass instruments, a glance at any of them will show that nearly all the increase in width of bore occurs in the last third or quarter of the tube—that is, the portion which eventually widens out into the bell. The trumpet is cylindrical for about three-quarters of its length, and the bell is about 5 inches wide. The horn is conical, except for about 3 feet in the middle, and the bell is about 1 foot wide. The tenor trombone is cylindrical for about two-thirds of its length, and the bell is about 6 inches wide. The cornet is practically cylindrical for about one-half of its length, and the bell is about as wide as that of a trumpet.]

One more illustration will be given in order to drive home the principles which have been explained. Everybody has heard bugle calls, and may have observed that they consist of five notes. The bugle is a rather wide-bored conical tube of about 4 feet 6 inches in length. The fundamental note (No. 1) is therefore B flat, and the five notes which are heard

are the harmonics Nos. 2, 3, 4, 5, and 6—namely, the black
notes of the following series :

Ex. 32.

The limited number of good harmonics (five) is owing to the
wide bore. The cornet and trumpet in B flat have the same
length of tube as the bugle, but the cornet has a narrower
bore, and that of the trumpet is still more narrow. The
consequence is that the bugle can be made to sound its fundamental note (No. 1), whereas that note is more difficult (or
impossible) to produce on the cornet or trumpet. The bugle
can also be made to sound the harmonics Nos. 7 and 8, but
with more difficulty than on the narrower-bored cornet and
trumpet.

The sum of the matter may be briefly put thus : *Wood-wind
instruments work entirely on the lowest part of the harmonic
series ; brass instruments work on all except the very lowest part
of the same series.*

The next step will be to enquire into the means adopted in
order to produce consecutive notes, which are lacking in all
except the very highest part of the harmonic series, or, in
other words, to enquire into the mechanism of wind instruments ; for it is obvious that no more notes can be produced
on a plain tube, and that, therefore, mechanical means must
be adopted to fill up the gaps.

Here the wood-wind and the brass instruments part company,
and each type must be treated separately.

SECTION IV

Wood-Wind Instruments : The Shortening-Hole System

The intermediate notes of the scale lying between the harmonics are obtained on wood-wind instruments by means of
what may for convenience be called the shortening-hole system.

It has already been explained that shortening a tube is
equivalent to raising its pitch. If seven flutes were made, the
longest being 2 feet, and the others each shorter and shorter
by certain amounts, they would, if their fundamental notes
were sounded successively, produce a scale from 2-foot C to B,
thus (see *a*):

FIG. 8.

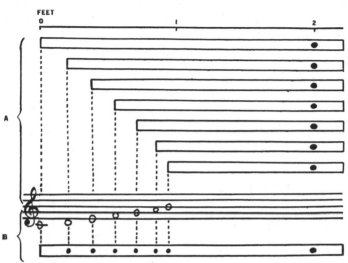

If holes were bored in the longest of these flutes at distances which correspond to the ends of the other six flutes, the same scale could be sounded if the fingers were successively removed from the six holes (see *b*).   Thus, it will be understood that opening a hole in a tube has the effect of shortening its sounding-length.   This process provides for the lower octave or primary scale on wood-wind instruments.   The next octave is produced in exactly the same way, but the wind pressure is increased so as to sound the second harmonics, an octave above the fundamentals (see Example 31, *c*) of all these notes.   The fingering of the first two octaves on a 2-foot wood-wind instrument can be diagrammatically represented as shown in Fig. 9.

All wood-wind instruments can ascend into the third octave above the lowest note of their primary scale, and in some cases can complete it.   The notes of the third octave are produced by various means which include the use of the third and fourth harmonics (in the case of the clarinet, the fifth), and the device technically known as cross-fingering; this will be referred to later.

The explanation just given shows the means of producing a diatonic scale on an imaginary instrument of 2-foot length, and serves to illustrate the shortening-hole system, and to show the six-finger-hole scale which is the original system on which all wood-wind instruments are based.

These instruments have, and have always had, an extension

downwards which gives one or more notes below the first note of the primary scale. In order to cover and control the extra holes required for this downward extension, keys have to be employed. These keys are simply levers provided with a flap at one end which covers or uncovers the hole, and they are operated by one or other of the two little fingers, or by one or other of the thumbs. Only on the bassoon are both thumbs

FIG. 9.

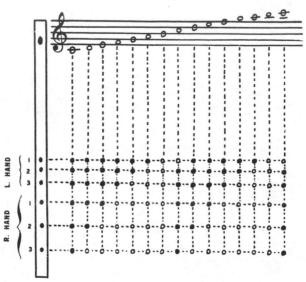

[The black spots represent closed holes and the hollow spots open holes. The two upper notes C sound more easily when the top hole, situated half-way along the sounding-length of the tube, is open. They could be produced with all holes closed.

When referring to fingers on wind instruments, the index finger is number one, the middle finger number two, and so on, just as in string-instrument fingering.]

employed; on the flute, oboe, and clarinet the right-hand thumb is used to support the instrument.

On p. 63 are shown the original six-finger-hole scales of the four main types of wood-wind instruments, together with the extensions downwards, and, in the case of the clarinet, the necessary extension upwards.

The case of the clarinet requires some further explanation. It was stated that this instrument sounds only alternate harmonics—namely, Nos. 1, 3, and 5; therefore, the first harmonic to sound after the fundamental is a twelfth instead

of only an octave higher.   The twelfth above the lowest note
E, is B ; this leaves a gap between the highest note of the
six-finger-hole scale and the B above, which is the first
harmonic to sound.   An upward extension of four holes is
provided, three of which are covered by keys.   The G hole
is on the under side of the tube, and is covered by the left-
hand thumb ; the key of the G sharp hole is controlled by
the second finger, the A by the first finger, and the B flat by
the thumb of the left hand, and in order to sound the third
harmonic (a twelfth higher) the uppermost B flat or
" speaker " key must be opened.   The primary scale of the
clarinet, including both the downward and upward extension,
is therefore from the lowest E to B flat.   This scale, on being

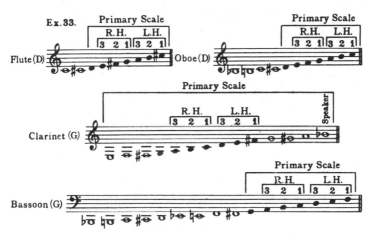

[The six-finger-hole scales are shown in black notes, and the extensions
in hollow notes.]

repeated with the speaker key open, and blown at greater
pressure, will sound a similar scale a twelfth higher.
So far the primary scale of these instruments has been
treated as a diatonic scale.   The intermediate semitones
require holes bored in between the tone-holes, and these have
to be covered by keys which keep them closed when they
are not required to sound.   On seventeenth and eighteenth
century instruments the chromatic semitones were only
obtainable by means of cross-fingering.   Cross-fingering
means covering a hole below the one which is actually sounding.   For example, on an instrument of which the primary
scale is D, if the F sharp is to sound properly, the E and D
holes below it must be open ; but if the E hole is closed and

the D and F♯ holes are open, an F natural can be sounded. The only semitone which can never be " cross-fingered " is the one which lies between the foot-end or bell of the instrument and the first finger-hole. This accounts for the early introduction of a keyed hole just below the first finger-hole on seventeenth-century wood-wind instruments.

Early in the nineteenth century all the wood-wind instruments had their complete system of chromatic keys, but had to wait till near the mid-century for the key system—generally known as the Boehm system—which has given them greater facility of execution in all keys, truer intonation, and the ability to play many shakes which were formerly impossible.

The essence of the Boehm system lies in a mechanical device, which will only be explained here in so far as it affects the lower part of the flute.

The problem was to get four holes, E, F, F sharp, and G, under the control of the three available fingers without having to move a finger from one key or hole to another, this movement being the principal drawback of the old system. Boehm mounted four keys covering the four holes on a common axle which ran parallel with the line in which the holes lay, thus :

FIG. 10.

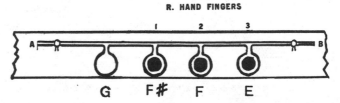

The three fingers lay on the three keys over the holes sounding E, F, and F sharp; these keys had hollow centres so that the " ring " could remain down without closing the hole. Being mounted all on the same axle (A-B), when any one of these three keys were depressed, the solid key covering the G hole was also depressed, and kept that hole closed. The four notes were produced as follows :

E : Third finger raised ; first, second, and G hole closed.
F : Second and third finger raised ; first and G hole closed.
F sharp : First and second finger raised, but third finger depressed, thus keeping the G hole closed.
G : Third finger raised ; this released the G key and opened the hole.

This device gave complete control of four holes by three fingers, and, incidentally, made it possible to bore the holes in the proper acoustical positions for good intonation, and of a size for the production of a good tone.

Modifications of the Boehm system have been introduced, and several other devices and systems have been amalgamated with it, yet the vital principle as described above holds good as the essence of all modern systems of key control on wood-wind instruments.

This brief explanation must suffice to show how, when it was similarly applied to other parts of the flute, twelve holes were brought under the control of eight fingers and one thumb.

The benefits of the system have been applied to oboes, clarinets, and to a lesser extent to bassoons. The pre-Boehm types of flute and oboe are now obsolete, but clarinets on the older system are still used.

The compass and transpositions of each individual wood-wind instrument will be described in Section VII. under their respective headings.

SECTION V

Brass Instruments : The Lengthening-Valve and Slide System

THE gaps between the harmonics on brass instruments are filled in by means of one or other of two devices, both of which are based on the same principle—namely, that of *lengthening* the tube and thereby lowering its pitch.

The lengthening-valve is applied to horns, trumpets, cornets, and tubas; the lengthening-slide is applied to trombones.

The former consists of three additional pieces of tube, one of which is long enough, when it is added to the main tube of the instrument, to lower the pitch of all open notes a semi-tone, another lowers the pitch a whole tone, and a third lowers the pitch a tone and a half (a minor third). These "byways" are let into the main tube, and each is provided with a valve or tap so that any one, any two, or all three of the additional tubes can be added to the sounding-length of the main tube. Each valve is controlled by a finger, and acts so that when the button or key is pressed down the air passage through the tubing includes the extra valve-tube,

and when released the extra tubing is cut off again. The
following shows a tube with the three extra byways or valve-
tubes, but does not show the mechanism of the valves:

FIG. 11.

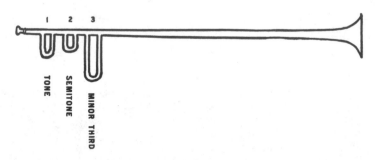

For a tube of 4½ feet (therefore in B flat) the length of the
valve-tubes would require to be :

> First valve (tone) : about 6½ inches.
> Second valve (semitone) : about 3 inches.
> Third valve (minor third) : about 10 inches.

The effect of the use of these valves will be as follows :

Valve No. 2 will lower the entire series of harmonics *one
semitone.*

Valve No. 1 will lower the entire series of harmonics *one
tone.*

Valves Nos. 1 and 2 will lower the entire series of harmonics
a minor third.

Valves Nos. 2 and 3 will lower the entire series of harmonics
a major third.

Valves Nos. 1 and 3 will lower the entire series of harmonics
a perfect fourth.

Valves Nos. 1, 2, and 3 will lower the entire series of
harmonics *a diminished fifth.*

Starting from any harmonic or "open note," and using the
valves in the order given, will provide a descending chromatic
scale of seven notes, including the harmonic. Reference to the
series of harmonics available on a brass instrument (Example
31) will show that the use of the valves will completely fill in
all the gaps in the whole series, except the gap of an octave

which occurs between the first two. Thus, a three-valve instrument will have a complete chromatic scale from a diminished fifth below the second harmonic to as high as it is possible to play. A moment's thought will also show that as the harmonics get higher and closer together the necessity for using the valves becomes less and less; further, that in the upper part of the series of harmonics many notes can be produced by alternative valves or combinations of valves.

The mechanism which is in general use to control the use of the valve-tubes is an arrangement by which a piston (hence "piston-valve") moves up and down in a cylinder. A few moments spent in examining the valves on a brass instrument will reveal the working of the device better than any amount of written explanation.

The following is the "fingering"—that is, the use of the valves necessary to sound all the notes in chromatic succession on a 4-foot brass instrument with three valves, starting at the diminished fifth below the second harmonic:

Ex. 34.

In the above the minims are harmonics, the lowest C being number two of the series which has 4-foot C for its fundamental note. It should be observed that a valve is used in preference to number seven of the harmonic series, which is slightly out of tune with the tempered scale.

The valve is simply a means of instantaneously lengthening the tube. Long before the invention of the valve early in the nineteenth century, crooks or shanks had been used to alter the length of both horns and trumpets. These are detachable bits of tubing of various lengths which can be added to the main tube by hand, and were very necessary because of the limited number of notes at the disposal of composers who had to write for valveless instruments. The addition of a crook or shank simply alters the series of harmonics just as a valve does, but the operation of changing a crook cannot be carried out instantaneously. Although the valve has to some extent rendered the crook or shank unnecessary, the latter are still used on trumpets and cornets because of the greater facility of execution which results from having the instrument pitched in a key with few sharps or flats in the key-signature. Indeed, both horns and trumpets are always made with detachable crooks or shanks, even though horn players of the present day rarely change their crook.*

The lengthening-slide of a trombone is mechanically a much simpler device than a valve, but its use has exactly the same effect—namely, that of increasing the length of the tube. Part of the trombone tube is made "double"; that is to say, an outer piece of tubing (called the slide) slides freely over an inner piece, and is moved about by the right hand of the player. A moment's examination of a trombone will show the simplicity of the device.

The slide can be placed in seven positions, and each successive position represents the lengthening of the whole tube by a semitone in pitch. Thus, the seven positions of the slide on a trombone correspond to the seven different lengths of the tube available on a valve instrument (that is, of course, counting the open harmonic as one), and have the same effect on the pitch of the instrument. Thus, if a trombone sounded C as an open note, the seven positions would provide a chromatic scale downwards to the F sharp a diminished fifth below:

Ex. 35.

In the above example the positions of the slide on a trombone are given above the notes, and the corresponding valves below.

Actually, all notes on a trombone are harmonics or open notes, because the slide is simply increasing the sounding-length of the tube, and is, therefore, altering its fundamental note each time the slide is moved.

It will be understood that a trombone will have a complete chromatic compass from a diminished fifth below its second harmonic up to as high as it is possible to play.

The whole may be summed up in the following example, which shows the harmonics (Nos. 2 to 8) available in each

* When an instrument is lengthened by means of a crook or shank, the length of each valve-tube must be correspondingly increased. This is done by means of a "slide"—*i.e.*, a part of the tube is double, so that an outer tube telescopes over an inner tube.

position of the slide. Harmonic No. 7 is again omitted on account of its faulty intonation:

Ex.36.

Trombone in
9-foot B flat

Positions 1st   2nd   3rd   4th   5th   6th   7th

(Harmonic No. 2)

[The fundamental note (harmonic No. 1) is not generally used on trombones, and is therefore not shown.]

The above provides not only a complete chromatic scale from E to B flat, but also some alternative ways of sounding the same note. Thus, the D above middle C could be played as harmonic No. 5 with the slide in the first position, or as harmonic No. 6 with the slide in the fourth position.

SECTION VI

REEDS AND MOUTHPIECES : ARTICULATION

THE sound-quality or tone-colour (*timbre*) of a wind instrument depends chiefly on the means employed to set the column of air in the tube into vibration. Whether the instrument is made of wood or of metal is a matter which affects the tone-colour but slightly, if at all; the shape—that is, the width of bore in proportion to its length—the shape and size of the bell (if there is one), affect the sound of an instrument rather more than the material from which it is made, but the main determining influence operates at the spot where the vibrations are generated, and that is at the mouthpiece.

Three methods of generating vibrations are employed on wind instruments:

Flutes sound by means of an *air-reed*—that is, simply a current of air directed against the edge of the mouth-hole (or *embouchure*), which is bored laterally near the head-end of the tube. The principle is the same as that of an ordinary whistle, only that the air-reed on the flute is not enclosed in any way and depends entirely on the lips of the player for its direction, whereas on a whistle it passes along a channel which guides it on to the edge of the hole.

The oboe and bassoon are sounded by means of *double-reeds*: these are two flat pieces of cane shaved at one end to a very fine edge, and tied together so as to leave a narrow opening

between the two shaved ends. These reeds vibrate between
the lips of the player.

The clarinet has a *single-reed*, also of cane and shaved to a
fine edge; it is fixed over an aperture in the mouthpiece so
that a narrow passage is left between the rigid mouthpiece
and the semi-flexible reed. In both cases it is the air current
which the player forces against the slightly elastic ends of the
reeds that causes the vibration, which is communicated to the
air column of the tube.

FIG. 12.

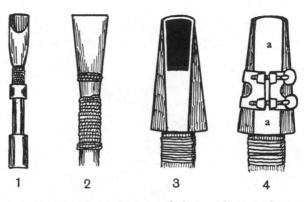

1 　　　　 2 　　　　 3 　　　　 4

1, Oboe; 2, bassoon; 3, clarinet mouthpiece without reed; 4, clarinet
reed (*a-a*) held in position by metal ligatures.

On brass instruments the lips of the player are the reeds.
A cup-shaped mouthpiece is pressed against the almost closed
lips, which are stretched over the teeth, and the air being forced
between the lips causes the vibration. It is the shape of the
inside of the "cup" of the mouthpiece that influences the
tone-quality on brass instruments; generally speaking, it may
be said that a shallow cup with an abrupt termination gives
incisive, brilliant tone, and a conical opening will give a
rounder, mellower quality. The two extremes are those of the
trumpet and horn, as may be seen in Fig. 13, while those of
the cornets and tubas are something in between the two.

The diameter of the cup at the rim will vary slightly according to whether the player wishes to command the higher
register of his instrument or the lower. Thus, a player of
higher parts, such as a first or third horn, or first trumpet,
will probably use a mouthpiece with a slightly smaller diameter

than that of the player of the lower parts.   The mouthpieces are, of course, all detachable, and generally fit on to the end of the crook or shank nearest the player.

FIG. 13.

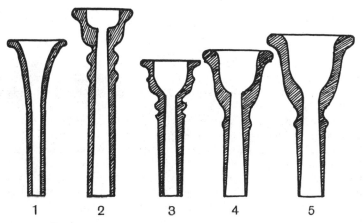

1, Horn; 2, trumpet; 3, cornet; 4, trombone; 5, tuba.

Players on wind instruments manage their breath and articulation in a manner not unlike that of vocalists.   The breath has to be taken in at reasonable intervals, and is gradually expelled, but should not be completely exhausted before a fresh breath is taken   Slurred notes will be played *legato*, just as on a string instrument, but separate articulation is given to notes which are not slurred; this is done by means of what is known as "tonguing."   The tongue interrupts the air current momentarily just inside the teeth, thus making what is practically the syllable *tu* (as in "tut") or *du*; this causes the slight break in the continuity of the sound which makes the difference between *legato* and *non legato*

A peculiar variety of articulation on some wind instruments is that known as *double-* or *triple-tonguing*.   In the former the syllables *tu-ku* are articulated rapidly; this makes a quicker repetition of notes than is possible by reiterating *tu*.   Triple-tonguing is similarly performed by repeating groups of *tu-ku-tu*.   Both are feasible, and most effective, on the instruments of which no reed or part of the mouthpiece is actually in the player's mouth; therefore, of the wood-wind, the flute is the only instrument really suited to this rapid variety of articulation. With a cup-shaped mouthpiece double-tonguing is always possible, but it does not come out well on large instruments owing to the slower speech of low-pitched notes. The small cups of the trumpet and cornet mouthpieces render this method of articulation very effective on these instruments.

SECTION VII

TRANSPOSITION

THE question is often asked, " Why not write the real sounds : why bother about transposing?" The answer cannot be given in a few words.

The technique of some wind instruments is such that execution in keys remote from the key in which the instrument is pitched is difficult, or even impossible. When there are two instruments of the same sort but of different pitches, the composer is always able to choose the one on which the execution will be practicable. Thus, the player must needs be prepared to play on one of two instruments which differ only in pitch, or, in the case of the brass, on instruments crooked in different keys. It stands to reason that the player of transposing instruments must have the same notation in his part for each of his instruments or crooks; he cannot, for example, be expected, when his written part is a scale of C, to play it as the scale of C on one instrument and as the scale of B flat on another! A pianist would not like to have to play a piece written in the key of C *in that key on one piano* and then have to play it *in B flat on another piano! The notation in the part must correspond to what the player actually plays on his instrument.* Hence, unless clarinet players are all prepared to play everything on one instrument, and brass players to use one crook or shank only, transposed parts must continue to be written.

The same situation exists when oboe players have also to play the cor anglais or the oboe d'amore; in fact, whenever one player must play on more than one instrument of the same type but of different size, there must be transposed notation.

It is sometimes argued that the real sounds might be written in the score, but a transposed notation in the player's part. Experience shows that the notes in the score must be the same as those in the parts : moreover, if this idea were carried out the work of transposition would not be done away with ; it would only be shifted on to other shoulders—namely, those of the copyist !

Conductors, in any case, must understand transposing parts, if only for the reason that the thousands of existing scores and parts would still remain in use, even if the millennium of "real sounds" were ever reached.

Students, although they understand transpositions, frequently have confused ideas as to whether the transposition is *up* or *down*. They may know that on a B flat instrument the written note C will sound B flat, but may be quite hazy as to whether that B flat is a tone lower, or a ninth lower, or a minor seventh higher than the written C. The following is offered as a means of clearing up any such confusion : Take C as a standard (any C will do), and know whether the instrument is pitched *above or below C*. When an instrument is *below* C, the written part must be *above* C by the same interval.

To take an example: A horn in F is pitched a perfect fifth *down* ; the part for an F horn must therefore be written a perfect fifth *above* the real sounds. Again, a clarinet in high E flat is pitched a minor third *up* ; the part must therefore be written a minor third *below* the real sounds.

The diagram on page 74 shows how orchestral transposing instruments are pitched, and what their transpositions are.

Examples.—An instrument is in A (down), *two spaces below* the central double line, which represents C or unison : the part for that instrument must be written at the interval and in the key *two spaces up*. A horn in D is pitched a minor seventh *down*—the eighth space down : the part must be written a minor seventh *up*—the eighth space up. The key-signature for a transposed part can be found by referring to the keys on the left of the diagram.

A few points in connection with transposition should be remembered :

(*a*) All the most common transposing instruments of the orchestra, except the piccolo, are *below* C, and the parts for them must be written *above* the real sounds. The high E flat clarinet is *above*, but is rarely used, and the old trumpets in F, E, E flat, and D are *above*, but are practically obsolete, though parts for them occur very frequently in the older scores.

(*b*) The horn in C is an octave *below* C, whereas the trumpet in C is non-transposing.

(*c*) All the saxophones, except the one in high E flat, are *below* C.

The foregoing is considered from the point of view of one

	Clar⁺s	Flutes	Oboes	Bassoons	Horns	Trumpets	Cornets	Strings	Interval
D									9th up
C		Piccolo							Octave up
B flat									Min. 7th up
A									Maj. 6th up
A flat									Min. 6th up
G									Perf. 5th up
F						Trumpet			Perf. 4th up
E						Trumpet			Maj. 3rd up
E flat	Clar⁺					Trumpet			Min. 3rd up
D						Trumpet			Maj. 2nd up
C									
B flat	Clar⁺				Horn (alto)	Trumpet	Cornet		Maj. 2nd down
A	Clar⁺		Oboe d'amore		Horn	Trumpet	Cornet		Min. 3rd down
A flat					Horn				Maj. 3rd down
G		Bass Flute			Horn				Perf. 4th down
F			Cor Anglais		Horn				Perf. 5th down
E					Horn				Min. 6th down
E flat	Alto Clar⁺				Horn				Maj. 6th down
D					Horn				Min. 7th down
C				Double Bassoon	Horn			D. bass	Octave down
B flat	Bass Clar⁺				Horn (basso)				9th down

who *writes* the score. For the reader of the score, the direction of the transposition is, of course, reversed. Thus, if an instrument is below C, the part for it must be read downwards. For example, a horn in E flat is pitched a major sixth *down*; to get the real sounds the reader of a score must transpose the part a major sixth lower than it is written.

SECTION VIII

Wind Instruments: Transposition, Compass, Notation

In this section only the most essential particulars regarding each instrument are given. No attempt is made to describe their technique, nor does their function in orchestration come under consideration; these belong more properly to textbooks on orchestration.   Percussion instruments and the harp are included, and are treated similarly.

Regarding the compass of wind instruments, the following facts should be understood : The lowest note of a wood-wind instrument can always be fixed, but the upward limit depends partly on the particular instrument used (make, keys, or extra facilities), and partly on the skill of the player.   The highest note, therefore, can only be approximately stated, and will be one which can be expected from ordinarily competent professional players using normal, but not exceptional, instruments.

The downward compass of some brass instruments cannot be so precisely stated.   In theory they can all go below their fundamental note by means of the valves or slides; in practice, however, only some can even sound their fundamental note ; therefore, the lowest note given will be that which is sounded by adding the combined length of all the valve-tubes (or the total length of the slide) to the second harmonic. Even then, as in the case of horns, the downward compass may exceed the effective or practicable limits of the instrument.   The upward compass is theoretically almost unlimited, and in practice is somewhat variable.   The highest note given here is that which can be expected with reasonable safety of good players under ordinary circumstances.

Flute.

The concert flute* is non-transposing, and the part is written on the treble staff.   The compass is three octaves (chromatic) from C to C :

Ex. 37.

the two highest semitones being difficult to play softly.

The eight-keyed instrument is practically obsolete; most English players use a Boehm flute.   On this instrument all shakes are practicable except the semitone shake on the lowest C, the tone shake on the lowest C sharp, and generally those above the highest G, which are either uncertain or impossible.

Double and triple tonguing is very effective.

* A bass flute in G occurs exceptionally, and is treated as a transposing instrument.

Piccolo.

An octave higher than the flute, and written an octave below the real sounds.   The *written* compass is from D to C :

The highest B is very difficult to play, and neither of the two highest notes can be played softly.

No shakes above the high G to A flat should be expected.

Oboe.

The part is non-transposing, and written on the treble staff. The compass is chromatic from B flat to F :

A few semitones higher may be reached by some players.

The Boehm mechanism is almost universally used, and on these instruments all shakes are practicable up to the high D.

Cor Anglais.

The same as the oboe, but pitched a fifth lower, and lacks the lowest key of the oboe.   The part is written on the treble staff a perfect fifth above the real sounds, and is given a key-signature in accordance with the transposition; thus, a piece in G major would have a cor anglais part with the key-signature of D major.   The *written* compass is from B to F :

sounding a perfect fifth lower.

Shakes above the high D should not be expected.

Oboe d' Amore.

A revival of the eighteenth-century instrument, and only rarely specified in modern scores.   It lies midway between the oboe and the cor anglais ; pitched in A, a minor third *down*, the part is written, with appropriate key-signature, a minor third *above* the real sounds.   It lacks the lowest note of the oboe, and therefore has a *written* compass similar to that of the cor anglais.

Shakes are as on the oboe, excepting the low B to C sharp and C to D flat.

[A barytone oboe, or heckelphon, is pitched an octave below the oboe, and occurs only in a few modern scores. Notation and written compass are similar to that of the cor anglais.]

Clarinet.

Two types are in use—the simple thirteen- or fourteen-keyed clarinet, and the modern instrument with Boehm mechanism ; the former in some military, boys', or industrial bands, the latter almost universally by orchestral players. Each player has two instruments, one in B flat and one in A, for which the written compass in both cases is—

Ex.41.

the notation, therefore, is a tone or a minor third above the real sounds, according to which instrument the part is written for. The treble staff and key-signature of the transposed part are used. A few notes above the high G are available, but should be regarded as exceptional. The composer selects whichever of the two instruments requires the key-signature with the fewest sharps or flats when the part is transposed. For example, a piece in F major would be written in G major for the B flat clarinet ; a piece in E major would be best written for the A clarinet, because the part would then be in G major with one sharp, whereas, if written for the B flat instrument, the part would have to be in F sharp major with six sharps in the key-signature.

Many shakes are impracticable on the older type of clarinet, but on the modern instrument all are possible from that on the lowest E up to the semitone shake on the high F sharp, although a few are awkward, especially those on the two lowest F sharps and on the two highest C sharps. The weak spot on the clarinet, both as regards tone and execution, is the part which lies between the top of the six-finger-hole scale (G) and the lowest note of the higher register (B).

Bass Clarinet.

Altogether nearly twenty different sizes of clarinet have been made and used at various times. Of these (excepting the common instruments in B flat and A flat) only the bass clarinet is frequently demanded in orchestral scores. One in C occurs often in nineteenth-century scores, but is now almost obsolete. The instrument in high E flat is an important member in the military band, and is a smaller replica of the ordinary clarinet. The E flat alto (a major sixth down) is now disappearing even from military bands, and its predecessor in F (a perfect fifth down), called the basset horn, will only be encountered in some of Mozart's scores.

The bass clarinet in B flat is pitched an octave below the ordinary B flat instrument, and is therefore a major ninth *down*. The notation is either on the treble staff a major ninth above the real sounds, or on the bass staff a tone above the real sounds; the *written* compass in the first case is the same as for all other clarinets, and in the second case an octave lower. On the whole, the treble staff notation is recommended—that is, a ninth above the real sounds.

Bassoon.

This instrument is non-transposing, and is written on the bass staff, with the occasional use of the tenor clef for high notes. The compass is chromatic from—

Ex.42.

although a few higher notes are possible.

It will be best, as an all-round rule, to avoid shakes below the lowest A, and above the A two octaves higher. Even within that limit several shakes are either difficult or ineffective.

Double-Bassoon.

The construction differs somewhat in various countries; in England it is usually made of wood with a fourfold bend of the tube. The part is written an octave above the real sounds, and the *written* compass is rather more restricted than that of the ordinary bassoon—

Ex.43.

although some higher notes are found in a few well-known nineteenth-century scores.

Shakes are hardly suitable to such a low-pitched instrument. Metal double-bassoons occur abroad, and are little else than bass sarrusophones, a group of metal instruments played with double-reeds, hardly known in this country.

Saxophone.

A conical-bored instrument of wood-wind type, but made of metal, and fitted with a reed similar to that of a clarinet.   The harmonics, and therefore the fingering, are like those of the flute and oboe.

Seven sizes, starting at high E flat (a minor third up) and going lower alternately in B flat and E flat, were originally designed, and of these the alto in E flat (major sixth down) and the tenor in B flat (major ninth down) have recently become prominent owing to their popularity in modern dance bands. Both are used in military bands, and have practically supplanted the E flat alto clarinet.

All saxophones are transposing instruments ; the parts are on the treble staff, with a chromatic *written* compass as follows :

Ex. 44.

The original compass was from B natural, but instruments are now made with the extra semitone.

The complete family is as follows :

Sopranino in E flat—a minor third *up*—written a minor third *below*.

Soprano in B flat—a tone *down*—written a tone *above*.

Alto in E flat—a major sixth *down*—written a major sixth *above*.

Tenor in B flat—a major ninth *down*—written a major ninth *above*.

Baritone in E flat—a major thirteenth *down*—written a major thirteenth *above*.

Bass in B flat—two octaves and a tone *down*—written two octaves and a tone *above*.

Contrabass in E flat—two octaves and a major sixth *down*—written two octaves and a major sixth *above*.

Shakes, like those on the oboe, are practicable, except a few at the two extremes of the compass.

Horn.

Natural (valveless) horns crooked in nearly all keys from high B flat to low B flat were used before the introduction of the

valve (see diagram of transpositions, page 74).   At present the
players prefer to use the F crook and take upon themselves
the responsibility of transposing the part when it is written
for some other crook.

The F horn is a 12-foot tube which can hardly sound its
fundamental note; the valves take the compass down a
diminished fifth below the harmonic No. 2, and as high as the
sixteenth harmonic can be reached.   Thus, the full *written*
compass of the instrument is—

Ex. 45.

sounding a perfect fifth lower.   That, however, must not be
regarded as the working compass.   The best and most useful
part of the instrument is that which lies between the *written*
notes G and G :

Ex. 46.

It should be noted that the first and third horn players are
accustomed to play the higher two of the four horn parts, and
are not expected to play as low as the second and fourth
players, and *vice versa.*

The parts are written on the treble staff, with an occasional
excursion into the bass staff when the notes are low enough to
require it.   It has always been the custom to write horn parts,
when in the bass clef, an octave below what would be written
had the treble clef been used.   Thus, the parts in the bass clef
for an F horn would be written a fourth *below* the real sounds
instead of a fifth above.   It is difficult to find any good reason
for this custom, or any good argument in favour of perpetuat-
ing it.

It has not been usual to give horn parts any key-signature ;
the necessary accidentals have always been written in the
transposed part when they were required.   Here, again, is
a mere survival of an old custom which arose from the fact that
natural horns could hardly produce any chromatic notes in the
key in which they were crooked.   There is no good reason for
not using key-signatures in parts written for valve horns.

The notes of a horn " speak " rather slowly, and, in consequence of this fact, shakes are not made with the valves.   Some
shakes, however, can be managed with the lips, and are most
effective when in the upper middle of the compass.

A few chromatic notes, a tone or a semitone below the "open" harmonics, were available on the old natural horns, and were used from early in the nineteenth century till valve horns became the standard instruments. These were produced by inserting the right hand up the bell (hence the term "hand horn"), and notes so produced were called "stopped" notes. This device is now made use of, not in order to get chromatic notes, but because of the peculiar quality of the sounds so produced. All notes can now be played in this manner, but are not very good when written below the third harmonic. When this effect is desired the part is marked "stopped",* or a sign (+) is placed over each note. A somewhat similar effect is produced when an artificial mute is put into the bell of the instrument. This is indicated by the word "muted" or *con sordini.*

Trumpet.

The modern trumpet can be put into either B flat or A by means of short shanks† (the straight equivalent of the bent crook). The tube is about 4 feet 6 inches long for the B flat instrument, and about 3 inches longer when in A. Another trumpet in C (4 foot) is used by some players, and is non-transposing. In either case the notation is on the treble staff, and the compass extends from a diminished fifth below the second harmonic up to the eighth harmonic. The *written* compass is therefore—

Ex. 47.

the part, when the trumpet is in B flat, being written a tone *above* the real sounds ; and when in A, a minor third above.

The fundamental note is not available.

The above must be regarded as the extreme compass, which, by lopping off a few notes at each end, leaves a working compass of from middle C to G (written) an octave and a half above ; within these limits most of the work is done.

The transposition of the older, and longer, trumpets is shown in the diagram of transpositions (page 74) ; it should be understood that the valveless trumpets in C, B flat, and A of Beethoven's time were based on 8-foot length, twice as

---

* German, *gestopft.*
† A valve which obviates the use of detachable shanks is often found on trumpets of the present day. The change can be made in a second or two.

long as the present instruments, and that their harmonic series
was that shown in Example 31 (*a*) (page 58).

Modern trumpet parts are usually given a key-signature, and
the choice of trumpet (whether B flat or A), also the key-
signature, is the same as for clarinets in the same two keys.
Players undertake the responsibility of transposing when they
play the old parts written for trumpets in other than B flat or A.

Shakes are made with the valves, and vary considerably as
to their practicability and effectiveness. The following are
best avoided :

Ex. 48.

A mute can be placed in the bell, and makes the tone faint
and rather echo-like.

Cornet.

All that has been written of the short modern trumpet applies
equally to the cornet, except that there is no cornet in C.
Otherwise, in compass, notation, and technique they are
identical. The difference between the two instruments lies in
the slightly narrower and more cylindrical bore of the trumpet,
also in the shallower mouthpiece, compared with the wider
and more conical bore of the cornet, and its deeper mouthpiece.
These differences in shape affect the tone-quality only. Since
trumpets have been reduced to their present small size, the
difference between the two instruments is much less marked
than was the case when long trumpets were used. At present
there may be more difference in the style of *playing* them than
in the actual sound of the instrument. The cornet is often
maligned because of a vulgar style of part which has for long
been associated with it, whereas the more refined past of the
trumpet gives it more dignified associations. However, as
nothing *can* be more vulgar than the treatment of trumpets in
present-day dance music, perhaps that instrument can no
longer afford to adopt a too superior attitude towards its plebeian
relative.

The bass trumpet found in some of Wagner's scores has
taken no permanent place in the ranks of the orchestra.

Cornets can be muted in the same way as trumpets.

Trombone.

Two tenors in B flat (9 feet) and one bass trombone in G*
(11 feet) are used in full orchestras of the present time.
Neither are treated as transposing instruments, so the actual
notes are written on the tenor and bass staves respectively.
The bass clef, however, is generally used when only one
trombone part is written, although that part may be played on
the tenor instrument.†   Both are given the key-signature of
non-transposing instruments.

The compass is from a diminished fifth below the second
harmonic up to the eighth harmonic, and is fully chromatic:

One or two notes higher are possible, and both *can* sound
their fundamentals (called pedal-notes); a few semitones below
the fundamentals can be sounded by means of the slide, but
these must not be regarded as part and parcel of the trombone's ordinary range.   Like all brass instruments, the best
part is that which lies between the second and the sixth
harmonics.

The slide of the trombone does not permit of a true *legato*
such as is possible on valve instruments.   Shakes are, of
course, not possible on slide instruments unless done with the
lips, and even then this is not an effect which can be counted
as a part of trombone technique.

Double-bass trombones have been made for Wagner pro-
ductions in both low B flat (an octave below the tenor) and in C.

Other trombones are the alto in E flat (obsolete), the bass
in F, and a soprano in high B flat which was used early in the
eighteenth century and has recently been revived for "jazz"
effects in modern dance bands.

Valve trombones have been made ever since the valve was
perfected, but have not generally replaced the more character-
istic slide instrument for use in orchestras.

Tuba.

Tuba is the orchestral name for the wide-bored valve instruments of the family which act as the principal bass voices in

* The G trombone is peculiar to England.   The instrument used on the
Continent is in F.

† Players on tenor trombones should be prepared to read from the alto,
tenor, or bass clefs.

military bands, where they are called simply "basses" or bombardons. The orchestral tuba in England is usually made in 12-feet F, although the part may be played on its nearest military equivalent in E flat, or even on the smaller B flat instrument known as the euphonium.

The wide bore and large mouthpiece of the tuba bring the fundamental note within reach, and an additional (fourth) valve, with a tube of sufficient length to sound a perfect fourth down, chromatically fills up the gap between the fundamental note and the augmented fourth above it. Theoretically the four valves between them give all but another octave downwards below the fundamental note, but for ordinary purposes that note may be considered the lowest. The part is non-transposing (with key-signature), and the compass is therefore

Ex. 50.

—for the F tuba, and the same a tone lower for the E flat instrument.

Shakes with the valves are possible, and are subject to the same valve difficulties as those on cornets and trumpets, with the added handicap that the low notes, of course, speak less readily.

Higher instruments of the same type, and one still lower than the military E flat bass, make up a family the members of which are only rarely demanded in orchestral scores. The following is a complete list of a group which appears to have grown out of Sax's original series of saxhorns, although all but one have discarded the family name. In brass bands a transposing treble-clef notation is still used, or, as an alternative, a bass-clef non-transposing notation for the lower members:

Sopranino (cornet) in E flat—minor third *up*—written a minor third *below*. ⎫
Soprano (cornet) in B flat—a tone *down*—written a tone *above*. ⎪
Tenor horn or saxhorn in E flat—a major sixth *down* —written a major sixth *above*. ⎬ Treble-clef notation.
Baritone in B flat—a major ninth *down*—written a major ninth *above*. ⎭
Euphonium in B flat (four valves)—a major ninth *down*, sometimes non-transposing.

Bass in E flat (four valves)—a major thirteenth *down*—
sometimes non-transposing.

Contrabass in B flat—two octaves and a tone *down*—sometimes non-transposing.

The last of these has been imported into the orchestra for a
few large-scale works.

The ophicleide, encountered in some older scores, was the
last survivor of the earlier *cornetto* or serpent family, and dis-
appeared soon after the advent of the tubas or bombardons.

Drums.

The two drums (*timpani*) have a nominal compass of a
perfect fifth each—

Ex. 51.

which may be slightly exceeded if the heads and screws are in
good condition.   Very tight or very slack heads, however, do
not give a quite satisfactory tone.   A third drum, occupying
an intermediate position, may be tuned from G to D, or, if
smaller, from A to E.

Key-signatures are not used in drum parts ; the tuning is
given at the beginning of a movement, thus: "Timpani in
A E"; and any change that may be required during the course
of a movement is stated thus : "Muta E in D," meaning, tune
the E down to D.   Accidentals are not usually written more
than once, and then only when the tuning has been changed.
Old scores and parts may have a transposed notation in which
the tonic of the key is always written as C, and the dominant
as G, the actual pitch of the two notes having been given at
the beginning of the movement.

The notation of the roll may be either *tr.* ∿∿∿ or $\natural$.   The
roll is played by quickly alternating strokes of the two sticks.

The following percussion instruments are those which
appear commonly in orchestral scores, and are not supposed
to sound a note of definite pitch : Bass drum, cymbals, side-
drum, and triangle.   The parts are noted either on a single
line or on a staff, and are usually, and quite unnecessarily,
given some clef, in spite of the fact that no pitch is represented.
Rolls can be made on any of these instruments : on the
triangle with the beater, and on the cymbals with either hard
or soft sticks.   The side-drum roll is made by alternating
double taps (a sort of rebound) with each stick.   Two parts

may be noted on the same line or staff by turning the stems of the notes upwards and downwards in order to distinguish one part from the other.

Harp.

The harp has seven strings to each octave, and these are tuned to sound the diatonic scale of C flat major. The mechanism, controlled by the player's feet acting on seven pedals, is such that each string can be raised in pitch by either a semitone or a tone. One pedal acts on all the C strings throughout the entire compass of the instrument, another on all the D strings, and so on up the octave. Each pedal can be placed, and can be fixed, in any one of three positions: these will cause the strings on which they act to sound respectively flat, natural, or sharp. Thus, it will be understood that if one C string is sounding C natural, all the C strings must sound C natural. It is impossible to have one C string sounding C natural and another sounding C sharp; but it is possible, for example, to have all the C strings sounding C natural and all the D strings sounding D flat.

Each pedal acts independently so that the player can alter the position of each one as he wishes, but he cannot, of course, move more than two at the same moment.

The compass of the harp is—

Ex. 52.

and the part is written, like piano music, on two staves, using treble and bass clefs just as is most convenient.

Each string can be made to give its octave harmonic by touching the string lightly at its half-way point; the lower part of the same hand which plucks the string is used for this purpose. The notes so treated are written at their normal pitch with an O over each note, the real sound being, of course, an octave higher. (See Example 17.) Harmonics are only effective in the middle of the instrument's compass.

PART III

SECTION I

A Short History of Conducting

The art of conducting, as it is understood at the present time, is little more than a century old; time-beating, however, has been practised by musicians, for the purpose of keeping voices and choirs together, for several centuries, and is much older than any form of organized orchestra.

Evidence that time-beating was practised even as early as during the Middle Ages may be found in altar-pieces, miniatures, and other pictorial representations of musical performances, in which a leader is usually depicted with a hand raised as if in the act of beating time. One of the earliest of these is a miniature which shows the Minnesinger Heinrich von Meissen (1260-1308) seated on a dais in front of which is a group of singers and players on instruments. In his left hand he holds a longish stick, and the index finger of his right hand is extended in a manner which suggests that he is marking time with that hand.

If pictorial evidence as to the prevalence of time-beating at such a remote period of musical history is a little vague and unsatisfying, the writings by musical theorists of the seventeenth century are quite clear and convincing; these prove beyond question that the singing of choral voices, especially when two or more choirs or groups of singers and instrumentalists were acting together, was commonly synchronized by means of either visual or audible time-beats. From similar sources information may also be gleaned as to the various methods of marking the beats: visual time-beats were made with the hand, a finger, a stick or baton, a roll of paper, a cloth or handkerchief, or, in one case (Caspar Printz, 1696), a handkerchief tied to the end of a stick; audible time-beats are described as having been made by stamping on the floor with the foot or with a stick; a peculiar method mentioned by Daniel Speer (1687) is that in which the time-beater hammered on an organ bench with a key.

All these devices, it should be understood, were used in connection with the rendering of ecclesiastical choral music, and by the organist-composers who occupied the most important and influential positions in the world of music up to the time when the further development of an independent instrumental style of music began to create a class of musician whose work was no longer devoted entirely to the service of the Church.

From the evidence of these early theorists it would seem that only two sorts of beat were known—namely, a down- and an up-beat. Only time groups of two or three beats were recognized (there was no provision for a group or bar of four beats), and in order to provide for a group of three beats the down-beat was made to last twice as long as the up-beat, or, as is shown in the following diagram by one Maternus Beringer (1610), alternatively the down- or the up-beat could be given double the time-value of the remaining beat :

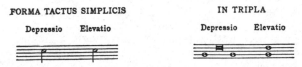

[*Niderschlag* = down-beat. *Auffschlag* = up-beat.]

Similar evidence is forthcoming in a work by Walliser dated 1611, and also shows how the down- and up-beats were made to serve for either duple or triple bars :

FORMA TACTUS SIMPLICIS   IN TRIPLA

Depressio   Elevatio   Depressio   Elevatio

In his preface to some Psalms for four choirs published in 1612, Viadana, an Italian Church composer who has been credited with the invention of the term *basso continuo*, gives some particulars regarding the duties of a time-beater when more than one choir are employed : he is to take up his position by the first choir, and from the *basso continuo* of the organist is to indicate the time and so convey it to the choir ; when the other choirs are to join in, he is to turn his face towards them, and by raising both hands give them the signal for their entries. Prætorius (1571-1621) also has left some directions as to the management of several choirs : each choir should be provided with a time-beater, whose sole duty it is to watch the principal time-beater, and to convey the beat of the latter to his own particular group of singers and players. An excellent representation of seventeenth-century time-beaters may be seen in the frontispiece of Prætorius' *Theatrum Instrumentorum* (1620) ; this shows very clearly three groups of vocalists and instrumentalists, each in charge of a time-beater, two of which are using the left hand to mark the time, while holding the music-book in the right hand.

The above, drawn from early seventeenth-century sources, could be amplified, but must suffice to show that it was considered desirable that a time-beating conductor should control the performance of music played and sung by groups or choirs at a time when written music was not even regularly barred, and almost before a style of music which could be considered at all orchestral, as distinguished from vocal, had become firmly established.

Audible time-beating appears to have been freely tolerated during the seventeenth and part of the eighteenth centuries ; in Paris it seems to have been regularly employed for the purpose of controlling performances of ballet and opera from the time of Lulli (1633-1687) until even after the middle of the eighteenth century. The story that Lulli died from the effect of a wound on his foot, accidentally inflicted with his " baton " while " conducting," may or may not be true ; if true, it points to the use of a heavy stick, and seems as if it were thumped heavily on the floor. From the complaints of later writers one cannot but accept it as a fact that some such distressing method of time-beating actually prevailed at the Paris Opera even as late as the time when Rousseau compiled his famous *Dictionary of Music*, published in 1768. Rousseau mentions a *gros bâton de bois* as the implement which so interfered with his enjoyment of the music, and another critic, Baron Grimm, writing in 1753, dubs the conductor at the Paris Opera a " woodchopper " (*Holtzhacker*). This inartistic method of keeping time also earned the condemnation of the one-time famous North German musician Mattheson (1681-1764), who puts it quite neatly when he supposes that choirmasters who mark time audibly with their feet are doing so only because they are more clever with their feet than with their heads.

Early in the eighteenth century it seems to have been felt that some improvement on the simple method of beating time, which employed only a down- and an up-beat, was due.

New and distinct plans for indicating three and four beats in
a bar are shown in some diagrams, dated 1706, by an Italian
named Tevo.   According to his plan, a bar of four beats was
shown by giving two consecutive down-beats followed by two
consecutive up-beats ; for a triple bar the plan was one down-
beat followed by two up-beats.   This method appears to have
become more or less standardized in Italy by the middle of
the eighteenth century, and is described by Rousseau in his
Dictionary as being the Italian method, whereas in France
(according to the same authority) only the first and last beats
of a bar were respectively down and up, any intermediate
beats being made either to the right or to the left, much
as they are at the present time.   The Italian method evi-
dently prevailed in England at a later date, for Dr. Busby
in his *Dictionary of Music* (1786) states that English
musicians followed the Italian custom ; his words on time-
beating are as follows :   "*Beating the time* is that motion
of the hand or foot used by the performers themselves, or
some person presiding over the concert, to specify, mark, and
regulate the measure of the movements.   If the time be
common, or equal, the *beating* is also equal : two down and two
up, or one down and one up; if the time be triple, or unequal, the *beating* is also unequal : two down and one up."
The reference to the foot rather suggests that audible time-
beating was still tolerated in England at that time.

The present-day method of beating time appears to have
originated in France early in the eighteenth century, and was
distinguished from the more commonly used Italian method
in that motions to the right and left side were used for all
except the first and last beats of a bar.   As early as 1702
a Frenchman named Saint-Lambert advocated a scheme of
beats for two, three, and four in a bar ; his methods for two
and three in a bar are identical with the present-day usage,
and for four in a bar differed only in that the second and
third beats were in reversed directions :

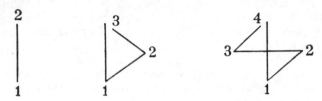

Some few years later (1709) another Frenchman, Monté-
clair, illustrated what is practically the present-day method,
thus :

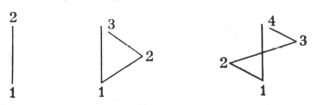

From the works of other French musicians which appeared
during the course of the eighteenth century it is quite clear
that the now standard methods of beating two, three, and
four in a bar were well established in France long before the
baton was used, as it is now, to direct all manner of musical
performances.   The following by Choquet (1782) is just
another way of showing the same plans :

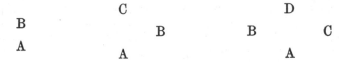

If it is impossible to say just when the Italian began to
give way to the French method, there can be little doubt that
when, early in the nineteenth century, baton-conducting began
to be generally employed for all purposes, the French method
of beating time was universally adopted.

Although time-beating was a recognized means of keeping
performers together during the seventeenth and eighteenth
centuries, it should be remembered that it was employed only
for the rendering of Church and choral music, and not for
purely orchestral music, nor for opera, except at Paris, where
audible time-beating prevailed.   The orchestral conductor,
like the purely orchestral concert, was as yet an unknown
thing.   Yet, during the course of the eighteenth century, the
earlier forms of purely orchestral music—concerti, suites, and
symphonies—were quickly developing and forming a class of
instrumental music which began to seriously challenge the
supremacy of the older vocal forms.   A means of directing
these orchestral works without any time-beating had in the
meantime established itself, and consisted of a sort of dual
control under the direction of a so-called "conductor" who
played on a keyboard instrument, and a violinist-leader who
gave the *tempo* and kept the orchestra together by means of
motions of his head and body while still playing the violin.
Thus, secular music was controlled by the joint efforts of a
"conductor" and leader who played on their instruments,
while sacred choral music was in the hands of organists or

choirmasters who beat time with their hands. The following from Koch's *Musikalisches Lexikon* (1802) puts the situation very clearly: " In Church music the Kapellmeister beats time . . . but in opera he plays the figured bass from the score."

Particulars of how eighteenth-century opera and orchestral pieces were thus " conducted " from the *cembalo* or piano in conjunction with the efforts of a violinist-leader or *Konzertmeister* are fairly abundant in the musical literature of the period.

All full scores, from early in the seventeenth till towards the end of the eighteenth century, were provided with a figured-bass part, which usually occupied the lowest stave of the score. The piano or *cembalo* player, who was called the " conductor," sat at the instrument playing the bass part continuously, and adding such harmonies as were dictated by the figuring; he kept a general look-out over the whole performance, giving a note here and there, filling up thin places in the orchestration, helping out and playing the part of any performers who went astray or missed their entries. His function was partly to give harmonic stability to the thin orchestration of the period, and partly to supply accidental omissions on the part of the performers. In the 1813 edition of Busby's *Dictionary of Music* the following appears under the article " Score ": " It is highly requisite to the conductor of any performance, in order to his knowing whether each performer follows his *part*, and to enable him to supply any accidental omission with the pianoforte or organ, at which he presides."

Several eighteenth-century writers have detailed the duties not only of the piano-conductor but also of the violinist-leader. All make it quite clear that there was no time-beating except that which the leader was able to give by motions of his head, his violin, or his foot. As a time-giver the leader was more important and probably shouldered more responsibility for the rendering than the piano-conductor. He was seated higher than the rest of the players, and was supposed to act as a sort of link between the piano-conductor and the orchestra. Busby outlines the duties of a violinist-leader thus : " A performer who in a concert takes the principal violin, receives the time and style of the several movements from the conductor, and communicates them to the rest of the band. The *leader*, after the conductor, holds the most important station in the orchestra. It is to him that the other performers look for direction in the execution of the music, and it is on his steadiness, skill and judgment, and the attention of the band to his motion, manner and expression, that the concinnity, truth, and force of effect, do in a great measure depend." All concur in allotting great responsibility to the violinist-leader, who, in spite of his being only a second-in-command under the piano-conductor, had clearly more to do with the actual playing and *ensemble* of the orchestra than the figure-head who sat with the score in front of him at the piano. It was the leader who had to start the orchestra playing, who had to steady them by movements of his head, violin, or body, who had to guide them at any change of *tempo* or pilot them through *rallentandos*, and who had to re-start them after a pause.

During the second half of the eighteenth century the violinist-leader grew in importance, while the piano-conductor gradually became less and less essential. The fuller orchestration of the period of Haydn and Mozart required less harmonic support from the piano, and the larger orchestras could not be so easily swayed by chords played on that instrument. With the eventual disappearance of the figured-bass part from the score began the gradual extinction of the function of the piano-conductor. The instrument relapsed into the position of being little more than a music-desk, and its player became an unnecessary and useless figure-head.

The period of dual control of the concert and opera orchestra was followed by an intermediate period during which the violinist-conductor became the sole leading spirit. Amongst such were Gluck, Graun, Stamitz, Cannabich, Dittersdorf, and a host of others who stood up in front of the orchestra, violin in hand, and by their playing and bodily movements urged their followers along, just as their successors did with the baton instead of with violin and bow. The race of violinist-conductors died hard ; the last stage previous to the advent of the baton-conductor was one in which the violin bow was actually used as a baton. Habeneck (1781-1849), the famous violinist-conductor of the Paris Conservatoire concerts, was one of the last of a type which lingered even after baton-conducting had become the firmly established method of directing all sorts of choral, orchestral, and operatic performances.

The first quarter of the nineteenth century, the period of Beethoven, Schubert, and Weber, saw the birth of conducting as we now understand the word. The conductor who stood up in front of the orchestra without any instrument, with only a small stick or a roll of paper in his hand with which he marked the beats of the bar, was actually a further growth of the violinist-conductor ; in short, the bow was exchanged for the baton. Continued growth in the size of orchestras and choirs, the development of a more complex orchestration, and the

higher standard of execution demanded by the scores of the
period, all called out for a leader and guide whose entire attention should be devoted to the control of a larger and more
complicated machine.   It is enlightening to know that in 1807
one Gottfried Weber, theorist and critic, wrote in favour of
silent conducting with a baton as if he were advocating something quite novel, and as if he were prepared to encounter
opposition.   Before the mid-century was reached the baton
had triumphed; orchestras, choirs, and opera were universally
directed as they now are, and a new type of musician began to
come into existence—namely, the specialist-conductor.

The pioneers of the baton were Reichardt, Anselm Weber,
and Spontini at Berlin, Carl Maria von Weber at Dresden,
Mendelssohn at Leipzig, and Spohr at Frankfort and Cassel.
Paris and Vienna lagged behind, remaining true to the old
style of violinist-conductors such as Habeneck and Schup-
panzigh, while London had to wait till 1820 for its first taste
of the new style.   Spohr's description in his own Autobiography
of how he introduced the baton at the Philharmonic Society
has often been quoted, but is worth repeating :

"It was at that time still the custom then that when symphonies and overtures were performed, the pianist had the
score before him, not exactly to conduct from it, but only to
read after and to play with the orchestra at pleasure, which,
when it was heard, had a very bad effect.   The real conductor
was the first violin, who gave the *tempi*, and now and then,
when the orchestra began to falter, gave the beat with the bow
of his violin.   So numerous an orchestra, standing so far apart
from each other as that of the Philharmonic, could not possibly
go exactly together, and in spite of the excellence of the individual members, the *ensemble* was much worse than we are
accustomed to in Germany.   I had, therefore, resolved when
my turn came to direct, to make an attempt to remedy this
defective system.   Fortunately at the morning rehearsal on
the day when I was to conduct the concert, Mr. Ries took the
place at the piano, and he readily assented to give up the score
to me and to remain wholly excluded from all participation in
the performance.   I then took my stand with the score at a
separate music-desk in front of the orchestra, drew my directing
baton from my coat pocket and gave the signal to begin.
Quite alarmed at such a novel procedure, some of the directors
would have protested against it; but when I besought them to
grant me at least one trial, they became pacified.   The symphonies and overtures that were to be rehearsed were well
known to me, and in Germany I had already directed at their
performance.   I therefore could not only give the *tempi* in a

very decisive manner, but indicated also to the wind instruments and horns all their entries, which ensured to them a confidence such as hitherto they had not known there. I also took the liberty, when the execution did not satisfy me, to stop, and in a very polite but earnest manner to remark upon the manner of execution, which remarks Mr. Ries at my request interpreted to the orchestra. Incited thereby to more than usual attention, and conducted with certainty by the *visible* manner of giving the time, they played with a spirit and a correctness such as till then they had never been heard to play with. Surprised and inspired by this result, the orchestra, immediately after the first part of the symphony, expressed aloud its collective assent to the new mode of conducting, and thereby overruled all further opposition on the part of the directors. In the vocal pieces also, the conducting of which I assumed at the request of Mr. Ries, particularly in the recitative, the leading with the baton, after I had explained the meaning of my movements, was completely successful, and the singers repeatedly expressed to me their satisfaction for the precision with which the orchestra now followed them.

". . . The triumph of the baton as a time-giver was decisive, and no one was seen any more seated at the piano during the performance of symphonies and overtures."

In the same year (1820) Spohr wrote of the Italian Opera at Paris as follows :

"I became confirmed but the more strongly in my opinion, that a theatrical orchestra, however excellent it may be, on account of the great distance of the extreme ends, should not be conducted otherwise than by a continual beating of the time, and, that to mark the time constantly by motions of the body, and the violin, like Mr. Grasset does, is of no use."

By the middle of last century conducting with the baton had developed the beginnings of a technique of its own. Gassner's *Dirigent und Ripienist* (1844), Berlioz' exposition of the theory of conducting at the end of his well-known book on Instrumentation (1848), the articles "Taktschlagen" and "Capellmeister" in the Koch-Dommer *Musikalisches Lexikon* (1865), Wagner's *Ueber das Dirigiren* (1869), and Deldevez' *L'art du Chef d'orchestre* (1878), all bear witness to the growth of a branch of musicianship which was rapidly assuming a separate existence, and was producing musicians who specialized in conducting only.

Very largely owing to the complexity of Wagner's scores and the growing popularity of his music, still more exacting demands were made on the technical skill of conductors during the last half of the nineteenth century; specialization was carried still further, and added to the necessity for a considerable technical equipment was a demand that conductors should also stand out as *interpreters* of music. The names of such as Liszt and Bülow, followed by a succession of Wagner specialists such as Richter, Levi, Mahler, Schuch, Seidl, and Mottl, introduce an era in which conducting had grown far beyond the confines of mere technical skill, and had developed what might well be called a virtuosity of its own. At this stage the personality of a conductor, the individuality of his readings, and his own interpretation of the music he directed, began to count for more than technical correctness. He was no longer only a time-beater, a mere technician; he was an artist playing on an orchestra as a virtuoso instrumentalist plays on his instrument.

The names of such as Nikisch, Weingartner, Lamoureux, Colonne, Mancinelli, and Safonof are only a few of a famous generation who were the immediate predecessors of the present race of star conductors. What they did for conducting is the equivalent of what Liszt and Tausig did for piano playing, and of what Joachim and Sarasate did for violin playing.

Within one hundred years orchestral conducting has grown from what can have been little more than mechanical time-beating to a highly complex art which requires such musical and personal qualities as are only rarely found combined in the same person. In addition to technical ability, experience, and sound musicianship, a conductor is now expected to show a personality which will colour every work he touches. His insight and sympathies must be comprehensive enough to enable him to deal with music in a variety of styles ranging from early eighteenth-century simplicity to twentieth-century complexity. He may be sensational, or he may be restrained and dignified, but he must never be dull and uninteresting.

It is well said of conductors that they should be born, not made; the student of these pages, however, will do well to realize that if conductors are *born*, they are never born *ready-made*.

SECTION II

Vocabulary of Orchestral Terms

English.	Italian.	German.	French.
Bass clarinet	Clarone	Bass Klarinette	Clarinette basse
Bass drum	Gran cassa	Grosse Trommel	Grosse caisse
Basset horn	Corno di bassetto	Bassethorn	Cor de basset
Bass flute	Flautone	Altflöte	Flûte alto
Bassoon	Fagotto	Fagott	Basson
Bass trumpet	Tromba bassa	Basstrompeta	Trompette basse
Bell	Campana	Glocke	Campane
Bombardon	Bombardone	Basstuba	Contre basse
Bow	Arco	Bogen	Archet
Brass instruments	Stromenti a fiato d'ottone	Blechblasinstrumente	Instruments à cuivre
Castanets	Castagnette	Kastagnetten	Castagnettes
'Cello	Violoncello	Violoncell	Violoncelle
Clarinet	Clarinetto	Klarinette	Clarinette
Conductor	Maestro di cappella	Kapellmeister / Dirigent	Chef d'orchestre
Cor anglais	Corno inglese	Englisches Horn	Cor anglais
Cornet	Cornetto	Cornett	Cornet à pistons
Cornett	Cornetto	Zinke	Cornet à bouquin
Crook	Corpo di ricambio	Bogen / Stimmbogen	Corps de réchange
Cymbals	Piatti. Cinelli	Becken	Cymbales
Divided	Divisi (Div.)	Getheilt	à 2
Double-bass	Contrabasso (old I. violone)	Kontrabass / Bassgeige	Contre-basse
Double-bassoon	Contrafagotto	Kontrafagott	Contre basson
Double stops	Doppio colpo d'arco	Doppelgriffe	Accords à deux
Double-tonguing	Doppio colpo di lingua	Doppelzunge	Double coup de langue
Down-bow	Arco in giù	Herunterstrich	Tiré
Drum (tenor)	Tamburo rullante	Rührtrommel	Caisse roulante
Drum (see Timpani)	Tambura	Trommel	Tambour
Drummer	Timpanista	Pauker	Timbalier
Drumsticks	Bacchette di tamburo	Schlägel	Baguettes
Desk	Leggio	Pult	Pupitre
English horn (see Cor anglais)	—	—	
Euphonium	Euphonio	Baryton / Euphonion / Bass Tuba in B	Euphonion

English.	Italian.	German.	French.
Fingerboard	Tastiera	Griff brett	Touche
Flageolet	Zufolo	Flageolet	Flageolette
Flute	Flauto	Flöte	Flûte
Flute (transverse)	Traverso	Querflöte	Traversière
Full score	Partitura	Partitur	Partition
Glockenspiel	Campanetta	Glockenspiel	Carillon
Gong	Tam-tam	Tam-tam	Tam-tam
Hand-horn (hunting)	Corno da caccia	Waldhorn	Cor de chasse
Harp	Arpa	Harfe	Harpe
Hautboy (see Oboe)	—	—	—
Horn	Corno	Horn	Cor
Kettledrums (see Timpani)	—	—	—
Keyed-bugle	Flicorno	Flügelhorn	Bugle à clefs
Leader	Violino principale	Konzertmeister Vorgeiger	Chef d'attaque
Mouthpiece	Imboccatura	Mundstück	Embouchure
Mute	Sordino	Dämpfer	Sourdine
Oboe	Oboe	Oboe	Hautbois
Oboe d'amore	Oboe d'amore	Oboe d'amore	Hautbois d'amour
Orchestra	Orchestra	Orchester	Orchestre
Part (orchestral)	Parte	Stimme	Partie
Percussion instruments	Stromenti pulsatilia	Schlaginstrumente	Instruments à percussion Batterie
Piccolo	Ottavino	Kleine Flöte	Petite flûte
Position (string)	Posizione	Lage	Position
Recorder	Flauto dolce	Plockflöte	Flûte-à-bec
Reed	Ancia. Linguetta	Rohrblatt. Zunge	Anche
Rehearsal	Prova	Probe	Répétition
Roll (drum)	Rollo	Wirbel	Roulement
Sarrusophone	Sarrusofone	Sarrusophon	Sarrusophone
Saxophone	Sassophone	Saxophon	Saxophone
Serpent	Serpentone	Serpent	Serpent d'église
Shawm	Scialumo	Schalmei	Chalumeau
Side-drum	Tamburo militare	Kleine Trommel	Tambour
Slide	Tirarsi	Zugstange Stimmstück	Coulisse

English.	Italian.	German.	French.
Slide trombone	Trombone a tiro	Zugposaune	Trombone à coulisse
Slide trumpet	Tromba da tirarsi	Zugtrompete	Trompette à coulisse
Stopped (horn)	—	Gestopft	Bouché
String	Corda	Saite	Corde
String instruments	Stromenti da corda	Saiteninstrumente	Instruments à cordes
String orchestra	Orchestra a corda da arco	Streichorchester	Orchestre à cordes
Tambourine	Tamburino	Schellentrommel	Tambour de basque
Timpani	Timpani	Pauken	Timbales
Tonguing	Colpo di lingua	Zungenschlag	Coup de langue
Triangle	Triangolo	Triangel	Triangle
Trombone	Trombone	Posaune	Trombone
Trumpet	Tromba. Clarino	Trompete	Trompette
Tuba	{ Tuba / Bombardone }	Basstuba	Basse tuba
Up bow	Arco in sù	Hinaufstrich	Poussé
Up-beat	Levata	Auftakt	Levé
Valve	Ventile. Pistone	Ventil	Piston
Valve-horn	Corno ventile	Ventilhorn	Cor à pistons
Valve-trombone	Trombone ventile	Ventilposaune	Trombone à pistons
Valve-trumpet	Tromba ventile	Ventiltrompete	Trompette à pistons
Viola	Viola	Bratsche	Alto
Viola d'amore	Viola d'amore	Liebesgeige	Viola d'amour
Violin	Violino	Violine. Geige	Violon
Violoncello (see Cello)	—	—	—
Wood - wind instruments	Stromenti a fiato di legno	Holzblasinstrumente	Instruments à bois
Wind instruments	Stromenti da fiato	Blasinstrumente	Instruments à vent
Xylophone	{ Zilafone / Sticcato }	Xylophon	Xylophone

SECTION III

BIBLIOGRAPHY

Historical.

CARSE: The History of Orchestration. (London, 1925.
CHYBINSKI: Beiträge zur Geschichte des Taktschlagens. (Leipzig, 1912.)
COERNE: The Evolution of the Modern Orchestra. (New York, 1908.)
KREBS: Meister des Taktstocks. (Berlin, 1919.)
*LAVOIX: Histoire de l'Instrumentation. (Paris, 1878.)
SCHÜNEMANN: Geschichte des Dirigierens. (Leipzig, 1913.)
VOLBACH: Die Instrumente des Orchesters. (Leipzig, 1913.)
VOLBACH: Das Moderne Orchester in seiner Entwickelung. (Leipzig, 1910.)

Conducting.

BERLIOZ: Art of the Conductor (extract from *Modern Instrumentation and Orchestration*).
BOULT: A Handbook on the Technique of Conducting. (London.)
CAHN-SPEYER: Handbuch des Dirigierens. (Leipzig, 1919.)
CARSE: The School Orchestra. (London, 1925.)
CROGER: Notes on Conductors and Conducting. (London.)
*DELDEVEY: L'Art du Chef d'orchestre. (Paris, 1878.)
*GASSNER: Dirigent und Ripienist. (1844.)
GEHRKENS: Essentials in Conducting. (Boston, 1919.)
LASER: Der Moderne Dirigent. (Leipzig, 1904.)
MIKORY: Grundzüge einer Dirigierlehre. (Leipzig, 1917.)
PEMBAUR: Ueber das Dirigieren. (Leipzig, 1907.)
SCHROEDER: Handbook of Conducting. (London, 1889.)
STOESSEL: The Technic of the Baton. (New York, 1920.)
WAGNER: On Conducting. (London, 1897.)
†WEINGARTNER: On Conducting. (London, 1906.)
†WEINGARTNER: On the Performance of Beethoven's Symphonies. (London, 1908.)
†WEINGARTNER: Ratschläge für Aufführungen Klassischer Symphonien. Band II.: Schubert und Schumann. (Leipzig, 1919.)
ZOPFF: Der Angehende Dirigent. (Leipzig, 1922.)

Orchestration (English).

BERLIOZ: Modern Instrumentation and Orchestration. (London, 1858.)
CARSE: Practical Hints on Orchestration. (London, 1919.)
CORDER: The Orchestra and How to Write for It. (London, 1895.)
FORSYTH: Orchestration. (London, 1914.)
GEVAERT: A New Treatise on Instrumentation. (London.)
JADASSOHN: Course of Instruction in Instrumentation. (London.)
KLING: Modern Orchestration and Instrumentation. (London.)
PROUT: The Orchestra (two vols.). (London, 1897.)
RIEMANN: Catechism of Orchestration. (London.)
RIMSKY KORSAKOV: Principles of Orchestration. (London, 1922.)
WIDOR: The Technique of the Modern Orchestra. (London, 1904.)

---

* Out of print and rare.   † Essays on style and interpretation.

MT   Carse, Adam von Ahn,
85   1878-1958.
C32
1971   Orchestral
         conducting